Péter Mujzer

The 38M Toldi Light Tank

KAGERO

The 38M Toldi Light Tank • Péter Mujzer • First edition • LUBLIN 2020

 • **ISBN978-83-66673-04-5**

Editors: **Péter Mujzer** • Photo: **Péter Mujzer, Fortepan, Páncélvadász.hu, Bonhardt Attila, Arsenalen.se, Yuri Pasholok, War Correspondent Company, Babucs Zoltán, Sárhidai Gyula, Szollár János, Service Manual, Virág Ajtony, Jean-Francois Antoina, Deák Tamás, Pálinkás Zsolt, Móker József, Karai Sándor, ECPA, Budapest Ostroma** • Maps: **based on original Army maps and OBs published in Csima János: Források a Magyar Honvédség II. világháborús történetének tanulmányozásához, Zrínyi, 1961** • Coloured original photos form cover: **Deák Tamás** • Line drawings: **Bajtos Iván** • Drawings: **based on original Army technical manuals** • Photo caption: **Péter Mujzer** • Color profiles: **Arkadiusz Wróbel** • Design: **KAGERO STUDIO**

KAGERO Publishing
Akacjowa 100, Turka, os. Borek, 20-258 Lublin 62, Poland, phone/fax: (+48) 81 501 21 05
www.kagero.pl • e-mail: kagero@kagero.pl, marketing@kagero.pl
w w w . k a g e r o . p l

The 38M Toldi light tank was the first modern armoured vehicle of the Hungarian Army; it was the backbone of the Armoured Troops from 1940 until early 1942. The photo probably was taken in 1941-1942, note the octagonal military insignia. [Mujzer Péter]

Introduction

The 38M Toldi light tank contrary to its designation entered into service in 1940. By the time it was the state of art in armoured weaponry of the Hungarian Army. Before that time the Army had its WW1 style armoured trains, armoured cars and the tiny Italian FIAT Ansaldo tankettes. The 38M Toldi light tank and its Swedish origin the L-60 were the same class as the German Pz. II, the Polish 7TP, the Soviet T-40 and T-60 light tanks, designated for reconnaissance and liaison role.

However, at the beginning of the war it was the only tracked armoured vehicles of the Hungarians to fight the Red Army in 1941.

Polish 7TP, the conventional light tank of its time developed from the British Vickers tank, its riveted hull and turret was common at that time. [Mujzer Péter]

German Pz. II light tank returning from the Yugoslavian Campaign with its three men crew standing around the turret, which armed with one 20mm canon and one machine gun, a typical armament of its time. [Fortepan]

The 38M Toldi light tank was also the first armoured vehicle produced by the Hungarian War Industry during the war.

The purchase and the license production of the L-60 reflect on the difficult position of Hungary at the beginning of the WW2. Hungary as the member of the Axis Powers could only choose between the neutral and axis states to purchase suitable armoured vehicles. The Germans did not sell the wanted armoured vehicles to the Hungarians; they needed for themselves to waging the war against the Soviets. Later stage of the war the Germans used the updated weaponry to blackmailing their allies. The Italian war industry could not produce suitable armoured vehicles. On the other hand the Hungarians gained very bad experiences with the L/3, CV-35 tankettes.

The only possible source was Sweden, the L-60 light tank of the Landsverk Factory. Sweden was ready to sell the license right of the L-60 to the Hungarians. After testing the L-60 the chosen Hungarian factories prepared for the mass production. At first with vital spare parts came from German and Swedish contractors, but the second series was built on Hungarian made parts.

During the war several developments and upgrades were tried and done, none of them was successful.

The 38M Toldi light tanks provided the backbone of the Hungarian Armoured Forces from 1940 to 1941. The 38M Toldi light tanks deployed in Transylvania, Yugoslavia and Ukraine.

The actual baptise of fire occurred in Ukraine in 1941, when it become obvious that the mobility and manoeuvrability of the 38M Toldi tanks were superior but their weapons and protection was inferior on the battlefield.

Even the light Soviet T-26 and BT-7 tanks had more powerful, long barrel 45mm guns than the 38M Toldi tank.

From 1942 the 38M Toldi light tanks were relegated to support and reconnaissance role within tank battalions and self propelled AA units.

The 38M Toldi light tanks served until the end of the WW2. Just two 38M Toldi light tanks, one-one 38M Toldi I. and II.A survived the war, captured by the Red Army and preserved in the Tank Museum of Kubinka.

Hungarian soldiers in early 30s dressed in the old standing collar uniforms. The officers and NCOs wearing their WW1 decorations, armed with 07/31M 8mm Schwarzlose machine guns. [Fortepan]

Hungarian infantry unit marching on a pared during the re conquest of Transylvania in September 1940. The troops still wearing the old 17M steel helmet dated back to WW1. [Mujzer Péter]

CHAPTER 1

Hungarian Army and Armoured Forces before WW2

At the end of the First World War, Hungary, as a member of the k. und k. Monarchy, ended up on the losing side. Her army disintegrated and her armaments were either taken over or destroyed by the victorious Allied nations. In 1920 the Allied Powers gave the Hungarian delegation their conditions for peace. This agreement, the Treaty of Trianon, was very similar to the one already imposed on Germany at Versailles. The main military aspects of the peace treaty were as follows: Military service based on contracted soldiers, conscription was forbidden, and the army was to consist of no more than 35,000 men. Training of officers was restricted and the existence of a General Staff was prohibited. The formation of Gendarmerie, Police and Frontier Guard units was also curbed. All war materials, which could be found, were confiscated. The existence or use of guns larger than 105mm calibre, tanks and all heavy armaments was forbidden.

Hungarian cavalry squadron parading in front of Viktor Emanuel III, the king of Italy in May 1937 in Budapest. The old cavalry traditions were highly regarded in the Army, but its size was much smaller than in Poland. [Fortepan]

The 37M 105mm light filed howitzer was one of the most modern artillery pieces of the Hungarian Army used by horsed and motorised version, called by the troops as "Göring howitzers". [Fortepan]

35M FIAT Ansaldo tankett was the first armoured vehicles of the Army, by 1940 was totally outdated, a machine gun carrier. The trooper wearing the leather two pieces protective cloth and Italian style crash helmet. [Fortepan]

The best design of the Hungarian War Industry, 38M Botond all terrain squad carrier truck manufactured by the Rába Factory, produced from 1940 until the end of the war. [Páncélvadász.hu]

The Hungarians utilised the motor vehicles of the Polish Army crossed the border into Hungary in September 1939. Polski FIAT 508 light utility truck used by a Hungarian signal company in 1940. [Fortepan]

Following Germany's example, the Hungarian Army began to organise secret units, and to conceal war materials, in direct violation of the dictates of the Trianon Treaty. These extra units were hidden in the branches of the State Police, Customs Service, Gendarmerie and other non-combatant governmental and non-governmental entities such as shipping companies and airlines.

During the secret rearmament, the Hungarian Army initially concentrated on enlarging the personnel strength and in building up a supply of the equipment forbidden by the Treaty of Trianon. Starting in the mid-thirties, Hungary had a chance to purchase weapons and armaments from Italy and Germany and from neutral countries such as Sweden and Switzerland. The home based military industry was also enlarged in accordance with the overall economic situation. By 1938 the Hungarian Army had seven mixed brigades, one cavalry division, (two hussar brigades,) an aviation brigade, an experimental motorised group and the River Forces. Under the direct command of the Chief of the General Staff were two heavy artillery battalions, four A/A artillery battalions, one signal battalion, one chemical warfare battalion, a mechanised transport regiment and an armoured group.

The total strength was 85,000 men, two and half times more than permitted by the peace treaty. 1938 brought a decisive change in the Hungarian Army's situation and development. Relying on the German-Italian alliance, and backed by the Polish and Austrian governments, the Hungarian Government revealed its rearmament program.

On March of 5, 1938, Prime Minister Kálmán Darányi announced his government's 1 billion Pengő rearmament program which, disregarding political and financial barriers, was aimed at accelerating the rebuilding of the national defence system within 3-5 years. This rearmament program dealt mainly with the enlargement of the mobile troops and the air force.

This plan provided a boost not only to the army but also to the country as a whole, generating many new industries and extra profits for the military industry. Recognition by the Little Entente states that, from their point of view, the international situation had deteriorated led them to negotiate an equal rearmament pact with Hungary, which was signed in a small Yugoslavian town, Bled on August 22, 1938. As of this time, Hungary's rearmament was legal. However, there still remained the problem of the impoverished state of the nation.

After the signature of the Bled equal rearmament treaty, Hungary speeded up the enlarging of its army. The former mixed brigades were expanded to form infantry corps, each with three infantry brigades. The final enlargement plan, called the "Huba Plan", called for the establishment of the following units by 1942:

25 infantry brigades, each consisting of two infantry regiments

1 cavalry and two armoured divisions
2 mountain brigades
1 frontier guard brigade
1 river forces brigade
2 air force brigades

GANZ Factory was the corner stone of the Hungarian heavy industry, producing rail stocks as well as military equipments, such as tanks. [Mujzer Péter]

CHAPTER 2

The Defence Industry in Hungary

According to the new goals of creating modern Armed Forces, the Hungarians had to establish a solid industrial basis to supply their forces with modern armament and equipment to be prepared to fight back the lost territories of WW1. However, it was not an easy task. Dominantly Hungary was an agricultural country with spares industrial resources and lack of raw materials. Due to the hostile environment and the preparation for the new war, the European countries were not keen to sell their weapons to Hungary. If so, these were out dated, weak designs which were purchased by the Hungarians as gap stop devices, like the Italian aircrafts, trucks and artillery pieces. The Germans used their war industry for black mailing their allies. This attitude just changed after 1942, when the Germans needed the Hungarian industrial capacity for their own goals. The German-Hungarian joint aircraft production started in 1943-1944 and delivered the Me-109 and Me-201 aircrafts.

Following the end of World War I, Hungarian military industry was in bad shape. The lost resources of her territories ceded to other nations, manpower losses caused by the war, and the limitations imposed by the Treaty of Trianon all played their part in this situation. During the late 1920s and early 1930s, the economic situation of the country began to improve. Hungary's economy was essentially based on agriculture, and those industries which existed did so mainly to provide tools and equipment meant for use in agriculture.

However, a small number of famous heavy industrial companies which originated in the old k. und k. period played a very important role in the military industry. From the 1930s, the Manfred Weiss, FÉG, Diósgyőri State Weapon Factory, Ganz, MÁVAG, Magyar Vagon és Gépgyár (Rába), GAMMA, and Danuvia companies provided the backbone to the Hungarian military industry. Due to financial constraints, these companies initially focused on repairs and modifications to existing equipment, but later worked on production under license and independent developments.

The Hungarian military industry was not comparable to the assembly lines of the German or Soviet factories, however still produced the third largest numbers of armoured vehicles on Axis side. [Bonhardt Attila]

The main building of the Army Automobile Depot at Mátyásföld in 1943, it was responsible for handing over the factory fresh armoured and motor vehicles to the troops, carry out the factory overhaul of the vehicles and supplying spare parts too. [Fortepan]

Production of Armoured Vehicles

The Manfred Weiss, Ganz, MAVAG, and Magyar Vagon és Gépgyár (Rába) factories were able to preserve and later expand their skills and capacities to produce armour for the Hungarian Army. Of course, in the early 1930s any work and development carried out had to be done in secret.

Having procured and tested the Fiat Ansaldo tankettes, the Hungarian military recognised that modern mobile-armoured tactics called for vehicles that were more powerful than these tankettes. Ideally a more powerful light tank was needed, but no such vehicle was being produced in Hungary and the Trianon Treaty precluded the purchase of foreign tanks. However, a Hungarian firm, the Manfred Weiss Company, offered a prototype of a light tank which was code-named V-3 (vontató = tractor) to conceal the real identity of the vehicle and its purpose.

Since Hungary possessed a developing heavy industry, one of the otions was to produce tanks domestically. The inventor Nicholas Straussler offered his new V-4 tank in 1937. The light convertible drive tank had an original suspension and was a further development of the V-3, which was developed in 1934-35 and received some interest from Japan and Britain.

In 1937, Hungary announced the comparative trials of three light tanks: the V-4, a PzI Ausf. A bought in 1934, and the Swed-

The Automobile Depot was responsible to supply the maintenance shops with spare parts for the armoured and motor vehicles. Spare pistons can be seen on the shelves. [Fortepan]

Engine maintenance at the Automobile Depot of the Army in 1942. Due to the extreme use of the motor vehicles for training and operation, the repair shops were busy to fix them. [Fortepan]

ish Landsverk L-60 which arrived in March. The V-4 armed with its 40mm gun was against a 20mm gun on the Swede and machinegun on the German vehicle. However the other characteristic of the V-4 were inferior comparing to the L-60 light tank.

The Swedish light tank won in the competition. The L-60 was simpler, and yet sufficiently progressive. Its chassis was the first to have an individual torsion bar suspension, the front armour was sloped, and the L-60 design had more room for further modernization. Straussler moved to Britain and worked with the Allies during WWII. His input into the victory over the Axis includes the Duplex Drive amphibious system used by American, British, and Canadian forces during the Normandy landings.

CHAPTER 3

Landsverk L-60

In the early 1930s the company of Landsverk had just established itself as a arms manufacturer. Landsverk had been an engineering company focused on producing railway and agricultural equipment. However in the mid-1920s Landsverk was bought up by a German company and became a way for German engineers to experiment with armoured vehicles designs banned under the Versailles treaty. Landsverks early work on armoured vehicles design had involved Studying the Raeder-Raupen-Kampfwagen M28 tank and building an experimental armoured car for the Swedish army.

In January of 1931 Landsverk was chosen over two competing companies to build 4 tanks under contract from the Swedish army. This would result in the Strv m/31 and Strv fm/31, two thoroughly modern tank designs which were some of the first to feature fully welded and sloped armour.

The same year a number of export designs were drawn up, ranging from self-propelled anti-aircraft guns to light tanks and tankettes. One of these designs was the Landsverk 60 or L-60 for short, which was Landsverks new light tank design. The L-60 was meant as a sort of scaled down Strv m/31 and would keep many of the features of that tank like the suspension and rear mounted transmission. There were even plans for a wheel-cum-track version of the L-60 called L-80.

But as the design developed a front mounted transmission was chosen and the leaf spring suspension was exchanged for a torsion bar suspension. This marked the first use of torsion bars on a tank.

The first Swedish tank was the licence production of the WW1 German LK II light tank, the Stridsvagn m/21. The LK II or the m/21 was the first tank serving in the Hungarian Army too. [Arsenalen.se]

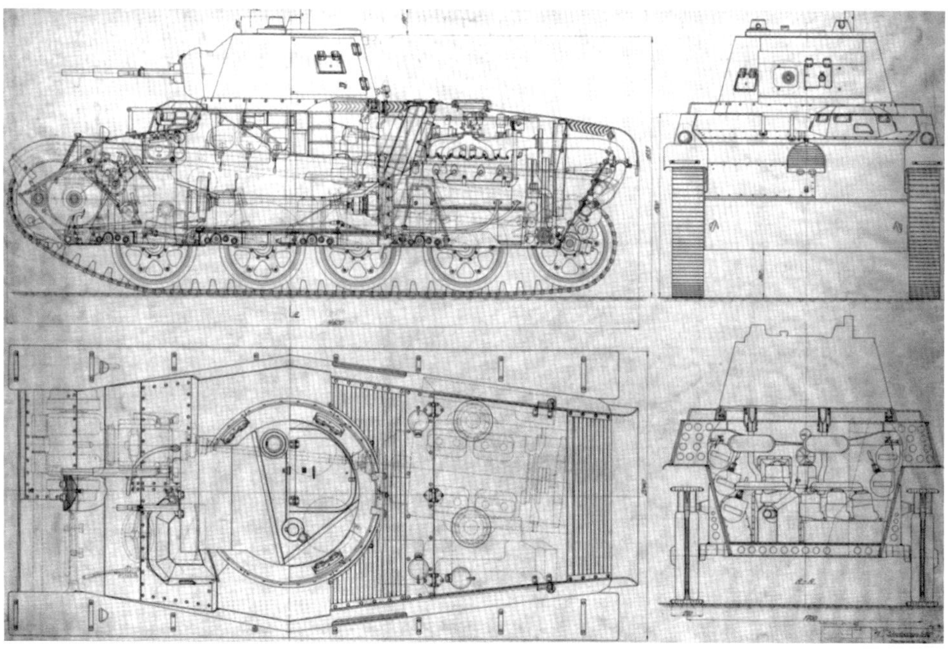

Technical drawings, cut way of the Stridsvagn m/38, L-60 light tank. [Yuri Pasholok]

Swedish Strv m/38, L-60 light tank, during the development of the light tank the engineers applied a new technical solution the torsion bar suspension. [Yuri Pasholok]

Winter exercise of the Swedish Armoured Forces with Stridsvagn m/37 and m/38 light tanks in 1940. [Arsenalen.se]

Stridsvagn m/38 tank. The tank regiment in Strängnäs had one of two tank battalions, but was still an Infantry regiment at the time. It became Tank regiment October 1942. [Arsenalen.se]

Stridsvagn m/38 tank in the Swedish Army, the military insignia painted on the frontal lower armour plate. [Arsenalen.se]

In 1933 the Irish Free State became the first country to show interest in the L-60 design and in May of 1934 two L-60 tanks were ordered by the Irish defence minister. However, the trial went wrong, when one of the tanks caught fire burned down. The surviving L-60 was to be delivered to Ireland. The Swiss military was also interested in the design but in the end, they decided to go with the Czech LTH design, which became the Panzerwagen 39.

The L-60 was a very good tank for its time. Its new suspension, small size and weight gave the tank excellent mobility and a top speed of 45 kph. The armament consisted of a newly developed 20mm Madsen automatic cannon and a coaxial 8mm Madsen machine gun which was better than comparable tanks at the time. In total, the tank carried 240 rounds of main gun ammunition and 3000 rounds of ammo for the coaxial gun. The main flaw of the design was perhaps the armour, which was only designed to be able to withstand .303 machinegun fires. This translated to a maximum thickness of 13mm for most of the hull and turret. The Irish L-60's would continue to see use until 1953 when they were finally retired due to a lack of spare parts.

While construction of the replacement L-60 was underway the Swedish army started showing interest in the design. A delegation was sent to study the vehicle in early 1936 and this led to mobility trials in June of 1936. Some minor changes needed to be made to the suspension and it was requested by the Swedish Army to add a commander's cupola.

An order for two Swedish L-60 prototypes was placed in July. These would be significantly reworked compared to earlier models. The hull was changed to fit a Swedish-built 142 hp Scania-Vabis engine and a new turret from one of Landsverk's armoured car designs was installed. There were also some minor changes like the expanded drivers position. The successful trials of these prototypes in August of 1937 led to an order of 15 production vehicles with a 37mm gun armed turret. Internally at Landsverk these were called L-60 S but they received the army designation Strv m/38. The deliveries of the Strv m/38 started in August of 1938.

Around the same time as Sweden started looking into the L-60 Austria placed an order for a prototype of their own. Unlike the Swedish version, the Austrian L-60 differed only a little from the original L-60. The earlier turret and engine was kept, though the enlarged driver's compartment was carried over from the Swedish model. Requests were also made for fitting a diesel engine but Landsverk managed to avoid this by claiming the tank had to be reworked to fit the new engine. This L-60 would later be sent to Hungary and serve as the basis for the 38M Toldi which would enter license production in Hungary in 1939.

38M Toldi light tanks lined up in the yard of the Army's Automobile Depot at Mátyásföld in 1943. On the left corner of the picture the turret of a German Pz. I light tank is visible. [Fortepan]

38M Toldi light tank was the backbone of the Hungarian Armoured Troops from 1940 until early 1942. The tanks had the octagonal military insignia which was used in 1941-1942. [Mujzer Péter]

CHAPTER 4

Licence negotiation of the L-60 light tank

The Landsverk L-60 tank was – in 1934, when it was designed – one of the most advanced tanks in the world and it was the pride of the Swedish industry. It was also available for export, but it wasn't too successful. First Hungarian contact with Landsverk happened in 1936. The representative of the Landsverk Company delivered a briefing for the selected personals of the Hungarian MoD, Chief of Staff, HTI and MÁVAG Factory on 25 October 1936 at Budapest. The Swedish briefed the Hungarians about their L-60 light tank, L-62 self propelled canon and L-185 armoured cars, which were ready for sale. In the following months, Hungarian company MÁVAG ("Magyar Királyi Államvasutak Gépgyára", Royal Hungarian Railway Company) negotiated the purchase of a test vehicle and plans for building this tank.

This resulted in the 1938 import of one L-60 to Hungary, where it was tested and compared to the locally designed Straussler V-4. As we know, the L-60 ended up as the winner of this.

For its time, the L-60 was very modern. The armour was mostly welded (riveted at some points too) and it was also sloped, increasing its effectivity. The suspension however was the most significant improvement, as it used torsion bars, not the old leaf spring systems, installed on many of its contemporaries. It was powered by an 8-liter Bussing-NAG L8V/36TR 155hp engine, allowing it to go as fast as 50km/h. It had a 3 man crew: the driver and two men in the turret, the commander and the gunner. Originally, the L-60 was to be equipped with a Madsen 20mm canon, but this was later changed in Hungary. Its main weakness however was the tankett-grade, 13mm armour. But it was excusable by that time. The tanks were still viewed as vehicles to fight enemy infantry and were expected to withstand only rifle and machinegun fire, but in WW2 terms it proved to be completely insufficient.

The representatives of the Hungarian MoD and Chief of Staff positively evaluated the L-60 light tank and supported idea of the MÁVAG to visit the Landsverk Factory, to inspect the production and the technical details of the tank. Based on the

Freshly painted 38M Toldi light tanks at the yard of the Automobile Depot in 1943, in dark olive-green camouflage with late style white cross military insignia and Mechanised Branch Sign painted on the turret. [Fortepan]

38M Toldi light tank belonging to the Light Tank company of the 1st Armoured Cavalry Battalion parading in front of admiral Miklós Horty, the governor of Hungary in September 1940. The position of the three crew members, driver-gunner-commander is clearly visible. [War Correspondent Company]

successful business trip, the MÁVAG wanted to buy a sample vehicle to continue the tests with the L-60 light tank. However, the Hungarians wanted a test run at Hungary and asked the Swedish to deliver a test vehicle to Hungary. The time line was tight, the Factory could not send a new test vehicle. Luckily the Austrian Army also tested the L-60 tank, which was redirected to Hungary on 17 August 1937.

The L-60 was tested with the Hungarian, home designed medium V-4 tank. The L-60 was superior to the V-4 on the field, but the V-4 was superior in protection and firepower. The HTI recommended both vehicles to put into service in the Hungarian Army.

From 21 October to 28 November 1937, the L-60 was tested again at Örkénytábor and Hajmáskér. The L-60 run 1751 kilometre without any technical problem, with top speed of 50kilometer/hour. The engine, shift, running gears, breaks worked in order. However, the steering mechanism, the truck like steering wheel was strange for the Hungarians.

Based on the test trials the experts of the MoD and HTI recommended the L-60 light tank for production and commissioning into the Hungarian Army.

At the end of 1937, the MÁVAG Factory in hope of the production contract bought the license rights and one L-60 light tank from the Lansverk Factory with modified turret. The turret was enlarged to accommodate radio equipment and provide bigger space for the crew. On the other hand the sample L-60 was similar to the original Swedish vehicles with its original armament. This tank arrived to Hungary in early of 1938. Later on this tank got the Hungarian number plate H-004. The Hungarians tested the new L-60 light tank

The tank number plate is H-456, the driver's position with its open armoured cupola and the searchlight of the 38M Toldi light tank is clearly visible. [Babucs Zoltán]

Inside photo of the driver's position, the 38M Toldi light tank had a normal steering wheel instead of the more common joystick. [Mujzer Péter]

Protective weapon shield of the 38M Toldi light tank's turret, weapons in protective canvas cover, and the machine gun shield had a cover plate which could be opened for ventilation. [Fortepan]

Detailed photo of the frontal view of the 38M Toldi light tank. Above the driver's position, on the turret are visible the machine gun magazine cover plates, the housing of the telescopic gun sight and a holding sleeve of the anti aircraft mount for the machine gun. [Fortepan]

The 38M Toldi light tank's turret had two side hatches situated on the left and right side of the turret, as well as a roof hatch for the commander. The arc shaped antenna folded down. Entrenching tool attached to the side of the hull. [Fortepan]

The gunner is embarking into the tank; its two pieces 35M leather protective suit was rather cumbersome to move inside the Toldi light tank. Behind the turret the engine deck is visible with the two round shape air filter opening. [Fortepan]

in March 1938, before the final decision on road Veszprém –Zirc- Győr.

The Hungarian military committee was quite satisfied, but recommended some changes to be made:

- The steering configuration be changed,
- The transmission be modernised,
- More extensive vision devices be added,
- The ventilation be improved,
- The suspension be modified for a smoother ride.

The insufficient armour and weaponry was also mentioned.

The commission recommended that four tank companies be equipped, each with 16 tanks, for each of the four mobile brigades (two motorised rifle and two cavalry brigades). Finally the licence to build the L-60 was purchased by the MÁVAG and Ganz Companies. The Swedish tank was designated the 38M Toldi light tank. The Ministry of Defence ordered 40 tanks from each company in February 1939.

Testing of the 20mm 36M anti-tank rifle of the 38M I Toldi light tank, the gunner position situated on the left side of the turret, the gunner aiming with its 38M telescopic sight. [Mujzer Péter]

The weapons – from left to right the 34/37 AM 8mm machine gun and the 36M 20mm anti-tank rifle – mounted on the gun bed, it had a traverse wheel/ turret drive mechanism. The magazines for the anti-tank rifle and for the machine gun were stored inside the hull and the turret.

In September 1938, these demands were evaluated by the MÁVAG and Ganz company representatives – some were rejected due to time constrains, because everyone wanted to start producing the vehicle as soon as possible. Regarding the armament, Hungarians had many options. The original Madsen 20mm gun from the L-60 was refused, because its design was

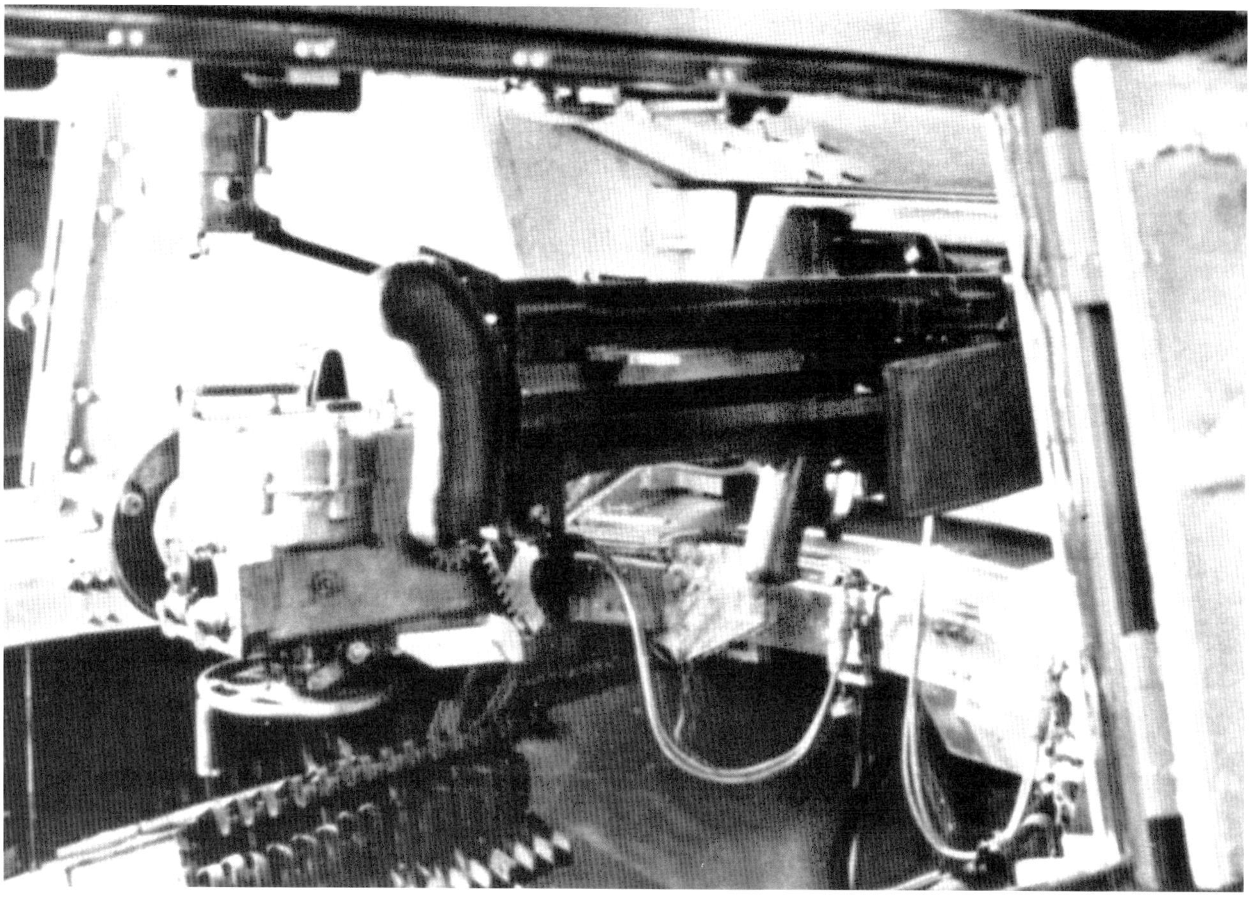

Right side view of the turret weapons with the 20mm 36M anti-tank rifle. Inside the turret was painted white. [Sárhidai Gyula]

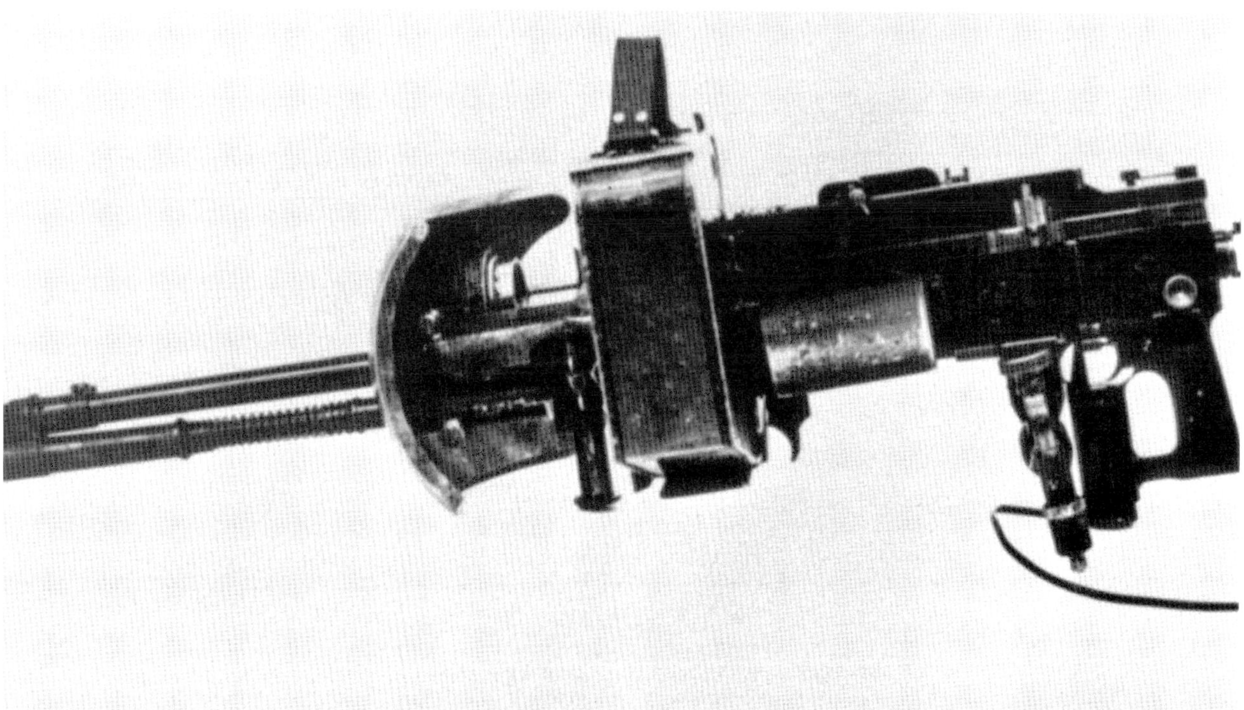

The belt fed 34/40AM 8mm machine gun of the 38M Toldi II light tank, it had the ammunition capacity of 3200 rounds. [Sárhidai Gyula]

too complicated for field repairs and no ammunition existed. Gebauer (Hungarian weapon manufacturer) prepared a 25mm gun project, but that proved to be unreliable. Other projects as the 25mm Bofors, 37mm Bofors and 40mm 37M (licensed Bofors) or 20mm Gebauer would (apart from also having reliability issues) require the turret to be redesigned and that was something no one wanted to get into. In the end, HTI (Hungarian Military Technical Institute) recommended using locally-produced semi-automatic 20mm anti-tank rifle as the vehicle's main armament. Essentially it was a license-produced Swiss 20mm Solothurn anti-tank rifle with some modifications (for example the 5 round ammunition clip proved to be too long, preventing gun depression and was replaced by a 4 round one). It wasn't a very powerful weapon: at 100m it could pen-

38M Toldi I light tank with arc shape radio mast and a holding sleeve of the anti aircraft mount for the machine gun. The weapons in protective cover. The vehicle had no military insignia just the Mechanised Branch Sign decal on the turret. [Szollár János]

38M Toldi I light tank, its 34/37 AM 8mm machine gun is in air defence position attached to the air defence mounting. However, the machine gun had no special anti aircraft sight and the magazine capacity of 25 rounds was not suitable against air targets. [Szollár János]

etrate only 18mm of armour, making it useless against anything heavier than armoured cars and light tanks. When engaging heavier tanks, all the gunner could do was aim for the enemy tracks and hope to immobilize him. The gun was paired with a Gebauer 8mm machinegun (34/37M), produced by Danuvia Factory in Budapest.

The Gebauer was already used at the Ansaldo tankettes with top-loading curved magazines. The machine gun was already installed into the turret of the Toldi tank, when it becomes obvious that it could not fire in negative angel, due to the location of its magazine. The belt fed machine gun was not yet ready for the Toldi light tank. An emergency solution was applied, the turret roof was cut out over the machine gun cradle and a small metal cupola was fixed over the hole to cover the machine gun's magazine. The first series of 80 Toldi light tanks were produced with this solution.

CHAPTER 5

Design and production of the 38M Toldi light tank

With such modifications, the L-60 in Hungarian service was designated to 38M Toldi. It was named after Miklos Toldi, legendary 14th century Hungarian warrior and hero, known for his strength. It was decided to mass-produce this vehicle

38M Toldi I light tank belonged to the 1st Reconnaissance Battalion is on display with troopers. Trough the open turret hatch the signal equipment is visible inside the turret. [Mujzer Péter]

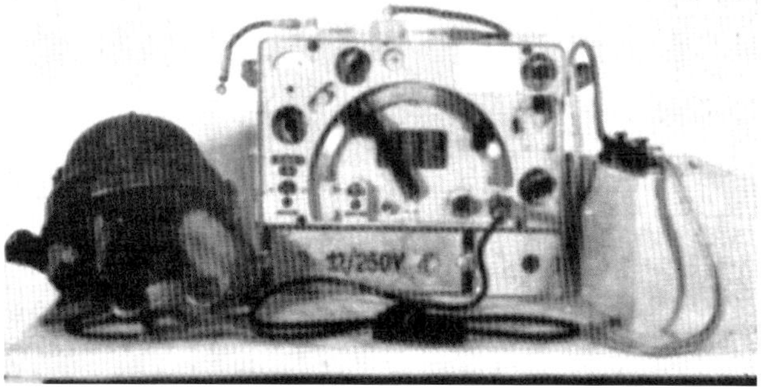

The R-5/a type radio equipment and the 39M crash helmet with earphones produced by Hungarian Standard Company was adapted for use on the 38M Toldi I light tanks. [Service Manual]

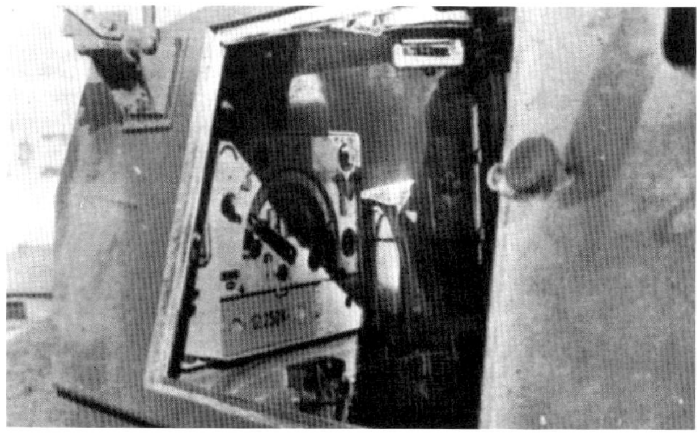

The R-5/a radio installed in the turret of the 38M Toldi I light tank used arc shape radio mast and the Toldi II had an R-5/a with stick radio mast. [Service Manual]

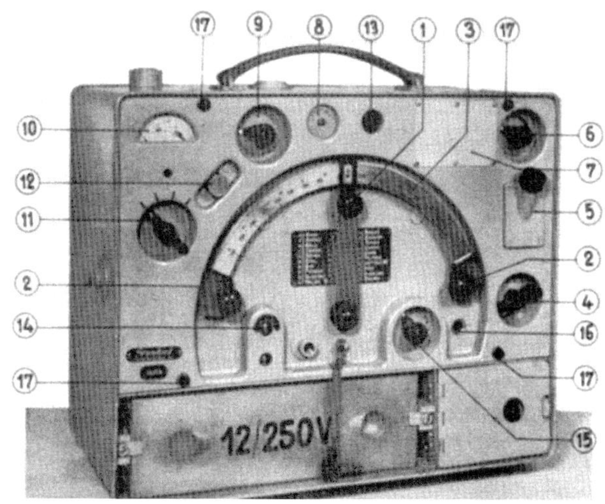

The instrumental panel of the R-5/a radio set. [Service Manual]

in Hungary, but mass-production was delayed by squabbles between the producers (MÁVAG and Ganz Gépgyár) and the army over the price. At first, the army wanted to order 64 vehicles, but it was decided at least 80 were needed and the order for 80 tanks was finalized on 17 February 1939.

Between February and September 1939, a prototype was built and components were tested: specifically the 20mm anti-tank rifle in the turret. Furthermore, locally-produced 38M R-5 radios by company "Standard" was implemented into the design. The range of the radio was between 2-15 kilometres in radio mode and 6-30 kilometres in mores mode. The first series had a half-circle band antenna, which was secured to the turret in two points. The antenna, when it was not used, laid and fixed to the roof of the turret. In case of signalling the antenna could be erected from inside of the turret. The second series got the stick antenna, situated over the right turret hatch of the turret.

The mass-production itself was initiated in autumn 1939 and the Hungarian army expected to receive first 32 vehicles until the end of the year. However, that was not to be, in 1939 the army didn't receive a single completed vehicle, as the production was halted by delays in components, that had to be ordered abroad. Specifically it was the Zahnradfabrik transmission, Bussing NAG engine, drive train components from Trelleborg Sweden, German Hosch torsion bars and Zeiss optics plus periscopes. This was considered unacceptable by the Hungarian army – it was decided that by 1940 all the components for the tank should be produced independently.

Designe of the 38M Toldi light tank

The shape of the light tank was very modern, like the late German Panther or Soviet T-34, of course in a smaller scale. The hull was 750mm long, 2140mm wide and 2020mm high, weighted 8,5 tonne, manufactured by welded technology.

Factory level engine maintenance of the 38M Toldi I light tanks at the Automobile Depot at Mátyásföld in 1943. On the rear of the engine are mounted fan wheels which provide cooling of the engine and the engine compartment. [Fortepan]

Workshop of the Automobile Depot at Mátyásföld, on the right side of the photo a 38M light tank, the engine compartment is empty, the engine removed for overhaul. [Fortepan]

The 38M Toldi light tank was powered by Büssing NAG type L8 V36 Tr, four-stroke 8-cylinder petrol engine. The photo was taken during the present-day restoration of the 40M Nimród Sp. AA vehicle in Budapest. [Bonhardt Attila]

The MAVAG Company began producing the German Bussing NAG engine had a displacement of 7913 cm/3 with the horsepower of 155 Hp. This photo was also taken during the restoration. [Bonhardt Attila]

The 38M Toldi light tank had 5-13mm thick armour barley provide adequate protection for its crew against heavier than infantry weapons, however the Soviet Army's anti-tank rifles were already proving to be an effective weapon against them.

At the rear and front armoured hull one pair of towing hooks was fitted. At the centre of the upper front armour panel is a searchlight surrounded by an armoured helmet with a bullet-proof protective grille at the front. The lamina can be moved, to operate the searchlight from inside the driver's seat by the driver. The searchlight slot also served to ventilate the brakes and power units installed in the front side of the vehicle. Underneath the searchlight position was an opening closed by screws, to adjusting the steering friction switch. Below this, a small oval cast with the vehicles' chassis number was attached to the lower frontal plate.

The rear armour plate of the 38M Toldi I light tank with mufflers, and the storage box on the left side with maintenance crew around the light tank. [Szollár jános]

Right side view of the 38M Toldi light tank, the track system with driven sprocket, road wheels and return rollers clearly visible. [Fortepan]

The drivers' position had a five sided protective armoured head protection cupola with 6 observation slots. Three of them were prismatic and three of them had bulletproof glass. These observation slots were protected by an inside-movable armour cover. When opened, the drivers' head protection cupola was raised on a semi-circular rail maid of spherical iron mounted on a sloping armour plate.

The rotating turret situated on the top of the armour hull, behind the turret was the ventilation hole protected by bulletproof grille to cool the engine and ventilate the combustion gases produced during firing.

The tilt tower consisted of the gun bed and the protective shield mounted on the outside. The weapons – 36M 20mm anti-tank rifle and the 34/37 AM 8mm machine gun – mounted on the gun bed so it could swivelled with the tilt tower, up +5 degrees, down 10 degrees. When the machine gun was disconnected from the anti-tank rifle, it could be moved independently vertically and sideways, both in +10 and -10 degrees.

On the turret roof, on the left situated the telescopic gun sight, on the right was the commander's observation cupola. There were five glass-prismatic observation slots on the dome's sidewall, which were locked with exterior-mounted, internally movable armour covers. Two additional observation slots equipped with bulletproof glass also situated in the commander's cupola, facing to opposite direction, also internally manageable armour plates. The commander's observation cupola has a hinged opening hatch; its size was similar to the outline of the dome. In opening position the hatch could be fixed, which provided a kind of protection to the commander standing in the turret.

The turret of the 38M Toldi I light tank, the commander's cupola with open hatch, the commander wears 39M crash helmet with earphones, on the hull entrenching tool and jack secured. [Szollár János]

On the turret roof, behind the armoured cupola of the telescopic gun sight, a holding sleeve was constructed to the anti aircraft mount for the machine gun.

Inside the turret, on the left side the aiming device was installed. The aiming device was mounted on the control unit support bracket so it rotated with the tower. In essence, it consisted of two gear units operating independently of each other but enclosed in a common housing, one for rotating the tower (sideways) and the other for vertical tilting the tilt tower (elevation). The turret rotation was controlled by steering wheel in two different speeds.

The commander and the gunner were seated on adjustable seats fixed to the turret ring, which rotated with the turret. In the rear compartment of the turret, which was enlarged by the Hungarian situated the R-5 radio set. The arch shape antenna of the radio set was fixed on the right side of the turret.

In the hull the engine room situated behind the fighting compartment. Behind the back wall of the fighting compartment a 60 litres water tank and the radiator was installed to cool the engine. The Büssing NAG type L8 V36 Tr, four-stroke 8-cylinder petrol engine located 5 degrees to the right of the vehicle's longitudinal axis.

The PTO shaft connected to the clutch mounted on the front of the engine travelled to the gearbox on the right side of the fighting compartment, below the floor plate, and then through the drive and steering gear at the front of the vehicle to where the driver shaft mounted.

On the rear of the engine are mounted fan wheels which provide cooling of the engine and the engine compartment. The fuel tanks were also placed in the engine compartment. The fuel capacity was 253 litres divided into three tanks (193+26+34).

Production

After commissioning the 38M Toldi light tanks, the Hungarian Ministry of Defence started the negotiation with the MÁVAG and GANZ Factories about the manufacturing cost of the tanks. Due to the short deadline the industry offered 125000 Pengő/vehicles price against the 100000 Pengő price offer of the Ministry of Defence. Finally agreed on the 110000 Pengő price and deliver the first 80 light tanks within one and a half year period, on the condition that the foreign produced parts of the vehicle will be delivered in time by the German and Swedish subcontractors. It was a serious condition, because the engines, gear shifts, running gears and optical devices come from abroad during war time.

First two 38M Toldi tanks were finished by February 1940, but the rest were still waiting in the plants for the components. Until June 1940, 20 vehicles in total were completed – by that point the timetable for the entire project was completely off, all 80 vehicles were supposed to be delivered by Spring 1940, but the latest estimates did postpone the production completion to March 1941.

The first two Toldi tanks, with serial numbers H-301 and H-302 were completed and assigned to the 2nd Motorised Rifle Brigade in April 1940.

However, the building program fell behind schedule and by June 1940 there were only 20 Toldis produced, and not all were fully equipped with armaments and periscopes. By September 1940, only 45 Toldi tanks had been delivered to armoured units; by October of that year the number had grown to around 72.

Meantime the crisis between Hungary and Romania, over the lost and disputed territories, reached the boiling point in summer of 1940. The Hungarian Army desperately needed the 38M light tanks as well as the 39M Csaba armoured cars to provide a credible threat to the much stronger Romanian Army.

The biggest issues that the production faced were delivery shortages of Zeiss gun sights, that couldn't be copied locally and were arriving only sporadically and in insufficient numbers from Germany. Torsion bars also proved to be problematic. The bars broke all the time and this issue was not fixed until local copies

38M Toldi I light tank had the climbing angle of 36 degrees, could step 0,6 meter and cross ditch width of 1,75 meter. [Mujzer Péter]

38M Toldi I light tank on cross terrain test, the weapons in protective canvas cover, the arc shape radio antenna is in transmission mode. [Mujzer Péter]

were produced by the end of 1940. Hungarian engineers did add their own solutions to the design as the production went on and as a result of this; the last models of the first 80 piece batch were somewhat different from the early ones. All the changes added to the vehicles were incorporated into the second batch later. To distinguish these versions, in March 1941, the first 80 vehicles were renamed from 38M Toldi to 38M Toldi I.

After the first 80 vehicles, the Ministry of Defence ordered a second series of tanks which were designated the Toldi II due to some slight modifications. This meant that the Toldi light tank became a 100% home-produced vehicle in 1940. The MAVAG Company began producing the German Bussing NAG engine, the Ganz Company produced the transmission, and the Ruggyantagyár Company manufactured the rubber wheel rims.

There were some difficulties in reaching agreement with MÁVAG and Ganz concerning suitable payment for the vehicles. The mixture of foreign and domestic parts also created many serious problems and resulting production delays.

In April 1939 the R-5 radio (built by the Hungarian Standard Company) was adapted for use on the Toldis. The Toldi I used the R-5 with arched shape radio mast and the Toldi II had an R-5/a with stick radio mast.

By June 1941, 85 Toldi tanks were completed in total, those from MAVAG bearing the serial numbers H301-340 and H381-385, and those from Ganz bearing the numbers H340-380.

Toldi II light tank

Toldi II tanks were practically identical to the late Toldi I series. The main difference however was the fact that unlike Toldi I, Toldi II tanks were built from parts, manufactured exclusively in Hungary. That finally solved the issues with German supply chain to Hungarian Army's satisfaction. Another change was the upgrade of

Driver position of the 38M Toldi I light tank with steering wheel and early style instrument panel. [Sárhidai Gyula]

38M Toldi I light tank belonged to the 51st Sp. AT-AA Battalion, behind the trooper on the right the cover of the engine deck is visible. [Fortepan]

Driver sitting on the fenders of the 38M Toldi I light tank/command vehicle of the 51st Sp. AT-AA Battalion in 1942. [Fortepan]

38M Toldi I light tank, number plate is H- 314, the drivers' head protection cupola was raised on a semi-circular rail maid of spherical iron mounted on a sloping armour plate, the searchlight and head lights with guards also clearly visible. [Virág Ajtony]

Cheerful civilians gathered around a 38M Toldi I light tank belonged to the Light Tank Company of the 1st Reconnaissance Battalion in September 1940, Transylvania. [Szollár János]

38M Toldi I light tanks without their main armament, wearing the late style military insignia belonged to the Armoured Training Camp at Esztergomtábor in 1943. [Babucs Zoltán]

the radio from type R-5 to R-5a. These vehicles were manufactured partially in parallel to the older Toldi I model (using German parts) roughly from March 1941 to the end of 1941. 110 Toldi II tanks were manufactured, 68 of which were made by Ganz (H423-H490) and 42 by MÁVAG (H381-H422). By the end of 1941, the Hungarian army owned 190 Toldi I and Toldi II tanks in total – because of the continuous upgrades with locally-built parts, later on these tanks were practically identical. The only way how to distinguish them was the old frame antenna of the Toldi I tank and the new straight antenna of Toldi II, but both models were soon upgraded to the R-5a standard and this feature disappeared.

38M Toldi IIA light tank

By the end of 1942, total production of the Toldi I and II tanks had reached 190 vehicles. However, the initial experiences in war had revealed the disadvantages of the Toldi: inadequate main armament and weak armour.

Command vehicle of the 51st Sp. AT-AA Battalion of the 1st Armoured Field Division, before the deployment at the town of Dorog, spring of 1941. Behind the 38M Toldi are Klöckner-Deutz trucks. [Fortepan]

The driver and the commander of the 38M Toldi I light tank, the commander had the 39M crash helmet with earphone, the driver had the 37M crash helmet without earphone. [Babucs Zoltán]

38M Toldi I light tank wearing the octagonal military insignia and the white lightning bolt unit sign of the 1st Reconnaissance Battalion is on display at the infantry barracks of Zalaegerszeg in 1942. [Fortepan]

Behind a Praga type workshop truck of the Automobile Depot is a dismantled 38M Toldi light tank, the frontal armour plate and the transmission gears removed as well as the drive sprocket and tracks. Behind the Toldi light tank are 39M Csaba armoured car and a captured Soviet BT-7 light tank. [Fortepan]

38M Toldi light tank drives on a cobblestone road, which worn out the suspension system of the tank. [Szollár János]

38M Toldi I light tank parading in a Transylvanian town in September 1940. The photo was taken on the right side of the vehicle, the axe and jack was attached to the side armour and the storage box is visible at the rear of the light tank. [Mujzer Péter]

This photo was taken from the rear left side of the 38M Toldi light tank with H-323 number plate, the storage box is visible and the spade and jimmy was attached to the side armour too. The anti aircraft mounting installed without the machine gun. [Mujzer Péter]

The 5-13mm armour was barely adequate against the infantry fire, the Soviet anti-tank rifles and any larger calibre anti-tank weapons could easily knocked out the Toldi tanks. The light tank's weapons, the 20mm anti-tank rifle and the machine gun were weak among their class of the reconnaissance vehicles too.

It was obvious for the Hungarian Chief of Staff from 1941 and ordered the improvement of it. The Military Technical Institute (HTI) began designing an improved version to satisfy the new requirements.

The Mod already planned in 1941 an up gunned Toldi light tank with 40mm gun. They wanted to order 280 new Toldi light tanks, 112 produced by MÁVAG and 168 by GANZ Factories. But the operational reports coming from the Mobile Corps in 1941 stated that light tanks could play just a secondary role in combat. The troops requested

Resting crew of the 38M Toldi I light tank at Esztergomtábor, belonging to the Light Tank Company of the 1st Reconnaissance Battalion. The field shovel is attached to the side armour. [Mujzer Péter]

38M Toldi II light tanks manoeuvring on a tactical exercise. The difference between the Toldi I and II was the radio equipment, the Toldi I had R-5 set with arc shape antenna; the Toldi II had R-5/a with stick antenna. [Mujzer Péter]

Light Tank Platoon of the 31st Independent Tank Battalion waits for the marching order at Jászberény. It was 9th Bicycle – Light Tank Battalion renamed to 31st Independent Tank Battalion, finally named 1/II Tank Battalion. The traffic control disc was used to communicate with hand signals attached to the pedestal of the anti aircraft mounting. [Babucs Zoltán]

Armoured troops returning from Transylvanian operation on rail transport. The 34/37AM Gebauer machine gun put on anti aircraft mount. The 25 rounds curved magazine had a vertical white stripe indicated that it is training/ dummy version. [Szollár János]

A nicely decorated 38M Toldi I light tank put on display at the Zichy Castle, Zsámbék 1941, wearing the octagonal military insignia and the Mechanised Branch Sign. [Fortepan]

heavier tanks and upgrading the armament and armour of the existing Toldi tanks.

The experts of the HTI concluded that the undercarriage of the Toldi could carry an extra 700 kilogram weight, but it was not enough to improve properly the armour protection.

The HTI delivered two options; a passive and an active to improve the Toldi tanks. The passive option was to reinforce certain parts of the armour; frontal plates from 13mm to 20-32mm, the turret side wall from 13mm to 25mm and the turret roof from 6mm to 10mm. However in that case the thickness of side and rear armour plates remained the same.

The second option was to improve the fire power but left the armour plates in their original thickness. HTI recommended installing the 40mm 37M tank gun, which was

38M Toldi I light tank advancing in Ukraine summer of 1941. On the both side of the turret one-one small opening window situated to provide ventilation. The octagonal military insignia was painted on the turret side hatch. [Jean-Francois Antoina]

Curious infantry and border guard officers and NCOs exploring with the turret weapons of the 38M Toldi I light tank at the out brake of the hostilities with the Soviet Union in June 1941. [Deák Tamás]

Tactical demonstration of the 38M Toldi I light tank for high ranking Hungarian Army officers in summer of 1940 at Esztergomtábor, the capability and capacity of the new light tank was not evident for the old school indoctrinated during WW1. [Szollár János]

Tracked armoured vehicles of the 1st Armoured Cavalry Battalion advancing on the training field. The 35M FIAT Ansaldo tankettes were unable to keep up with the 38M Toldi I light tanks, especially on difficult terrain. [Mujzer Péter]

Bottom frontal view of the 38M Toldi I light tank, the big size octagonal military insignia was painted exactly on the driver's position which made a perfect aiming point for the enemy anti-tank gunners. [Mujzer Péter]

38M Toldi I light tank belonged to the 9th Bicycle – Light Tank Battalion in spring 1941, no militray insignia, just the Mechanised Branch Sign decal is on the turret. [Babucs Zoltán]

38M Toldi I light tank belonged to the Light Tank Company of the 1st Reconnaissance Battalion. On the turret the machine gun cover plate and one of the turret apertures opened to help the ventilation inside the turret. [Mujzer Péter]

developed for the Hungarian V-4 experimental tank. The H-434 number plated Toldi I. was used for the experiment, its tilt tower, gun mantel, gun shield were replaced. The tests were done in the winter of 1941-1942, which prove that the new gun, improvement of the frontal armour from 13mm to 20-35mm and a new steering mechanism caused 500 kilogram weight increase.

The new vehicle had additional armour on the front of the hull and on the turret, and was to be armed with a 40mm gun. Two prototypes were completed but production was delayed

The 38M Toldi I light tank had very thin armour, which on impact of an armoured-piercing shell easily penetrated. Luckily the AP shells did not blow inside the turret just went through it. This is the internal damage what caused by a Soviet anti-tank round, definitely killing the turret crew, in 1941 the 38M Toldi I light tank belonged to the 9th Tank Battalion. [Babucs Zoltán]

The same tank turret of the 38M Toldi I light tank from outside. The big size and colourful military insignia was a perfect aiming point. [Babucs Zoltán]

due to work on rebuilding the earlier Toldi tanks and work on the Turán program.

The new improved Toldi light tank variant was called 38M Toldi IIA. The main reason for its existence was the fact the original 38M Toldi was outclassed even by Soviet light tanks, that were resistant to its 20mm anti-tank rifle. In order to improve that, the designers tried to replace the weapon with something more powerful. In 1942 a prototype was made, where the 36M 20mm anti-tank rifle was replaced by a 37/42M MÁVAG tank gun. It basically was a shorter version of the original 40mm 37M gun (used at the Straussler V-4 tank), which in turn was a licensed 40mm Bofors. It was a 40mm L/45 gun with muzzle velocity of 800 m/s and the rate of fire 16 rounds per minute. The shell (originally designed for Bofors AA canon) could penetrate 64mm of armour (30 degree slope) at 100 meters and 30mm of armour (same slope) at 1000m, however by 1944 this too proved to be inadequate. The gun shield armour was improved to 35mm, with special protective armour sleeve on the gun barrel and steel cover on the machine gun barrel.

The machinegun was also replaced by a later model belt-fed 8mm Gebauer 34/40AM.

Due to the size of the weapon, the turret was modified. A metal box was attached to the rear of the turret to give better stability. The box was made of 13-20mm thick armour plates and opened on the top and used for storage space for the crew or spare parts.

The armour plates were only strengthening on the front hull from 13mm to 23-35mm. The maintenance hatches were closed by armour plates and the searchlight was removed.

The armour was increased and the torsion was strengthened. The 80 tanks so modified were designated Toldi II A. As 1 October 1943 the armoured forces had 96 Toldi T20 and 80

The prototype of the 38M Toldi II light tank armed with 40mm gun parking on the yard of the MÁVAG Factory. The experimental vehicle had the H-434 number plate. [Sárhidai Gyula]

Prototype version of the 38M Toldi II light tank with experimental skirt plates, a metal box was attached to the rear of the turret to keep the balance of the new gun. [Sárhidai Gyula]

Toldi T40 tanks. The T20 and T40 reflected on the calibre of their main weapons.

Based on German experience, the HTI also experimented with a skirting-plated Toldi tank in 1943. An up-gunned Toldi II A, number plate H-423, was covered with four 380x107cm, 5mm non perforated additional armour plates, but tests showed that this did not provide better protection but merely increased the weight by 500kg.

Later on, at the Turán tanks and Zrínyi assault howitzers, the Hungarian used perforated armour skirts. It was lighter and the perforated armour plates could deflect the Soviet anti-tank rifle shots.

Despite the prototype being available in 1942, the conversion process was incredibly slow. Eighty vehicles were converted (mostly from Toldi II tanks) to carry the new gun, but due to inexplicable delays, the whole program was really slow – the conversion started in early 1943, but ended as late as 1944. Probably, by that time the medium and heavy Turán tank program was the priority and the army also recognised how outdated was the Toldi, even with the 40mm gun against the Soviet T-34 tanks.

38M Toldi III light tank

In 1943, Hungarian engineers developed a new tank that would replace the 38M as the new light tank. The new tank was indexed 38M Toldi III. Original 220 tanks were ordered but later it was reduced to 40 vehicles.

The Hungarian designers were severely limited in the attempt to increase the protection of the Toldi light tank by two factors. First was obviously the weight. Second was the ground pressure – Toldi had relatively thin tracks and if too heavy, the terrain passability would suffer too much. Ganz Company proposed a Toldi variant compromise with the increased armour: 35mm in the front (both turret and hull), 25mm turret sides and 20mm hull sides. Apart from the fact the armour was now thicker, the turret (armed with the same gun as Toldi IIA) was made longer. The army was not satisfied, but despite the refusal, Ganz converted two prototypes in spring 1942 from exiting Toldi IIA tanks. Its armour remained at the level of its predecessor, but could be equipped with side skirts, tested on the Toldi IIA. They could not save the tank from shells, but were a serious impediment to infantry anti-tank rifles.

A new turret was developed for the Toldi III, it was 50mm higher than the original turret, to provide fee fire between -10 and +25 degrees for the 37/40M tank gun. Instead of the attached metal box at the rear of the turret, the turret was enlarged. The turret frontal armour increased to 35mm, the turret roof to 10mm. The frontal armour increased to 20, later 35mm. The rear armour also increased to 10mm.

This modification changed the original 8,5 ton to 9,45 ton and the speed reduced to 45 km/h.

Between June 1942 and March 1943, the prototypes were tested. Ganz was ready to produce 40 vehicles of this type, but the army approved only twelve, that ended up in various states of assembly. Some sources state that all 12 were finished, while other sources state only 3 were ever finished from September 1943 to 1944. In summer of 1944 the GANZ Factory still reported that the 12 tanks unfinished due to the missing engines, armour plates and spare parts. The unfinished vehicles remained at the GANZ Factory and were scrapped in 1954. What is clear however is that the project had lower priority than the Toldi IIA conversions.

Production of the 43M Toldi III began at Ganz in the autumn of 1943 but there is no record of how many, if any, were delivered to the armoured troops.

On 2 July, 1944, Allied aircraft delivered a massive bomb strike on Budapest, which crippled Ganz Factories.

43M Toldi medical tank

Battlefield experiences highlighted the lack of armoured medical vehicles. In 1942 the 30th Tank Regiment successfully used three 38M Toldi II for transporting medical crews close to damaged tanks to evacuate injured personnel from the battle field.

The HTI recommended the modification of a few Toldi I tanks for medical duties. In March 1944 nine Toldi I were modified at Ganz. The left side hatch was enlarging to ease boarding casualties and the amount of ammunition carried was reduced and instead of ammunition boxes, medical materials were kept in the turret. The nine medical vehicles, named 43. M Toldi medical light tanks were handed over to the troops in June - July 1944. The known number plates are H-318, H-347, H-356, H-358, the other five remained unknown.

Toldi tank hunter vehicle

The 38M Toldi I light tanks, produced from 1939 to 1940, became completely obsolete and lost most of their combat value by 1944 with their 20mm Solothurn anti-tank rifle and only 13mm thin frontal armour. But, because of their relatively weak suspension, it was not possible to upgrade them with thicker armour and to mount an enlarged turret with a stronger 40mm gun on them like on the 38M Toldi IIA light tanks, because their weak torsion bars just could not bear the additional weight.

However, 38M Toldi I tanks could not be upgraded, the Hungarian engineers had to figure out a different way to make the Toldi I useful again. One idea was to make a similar design to the German Marder series of tank destroyers on the chassis of the 38M Toldi I.

In 1942-43, the Wehrmacht handed over 7 Marder II tank destroyers (for temporary use, without crew) to the 1st Armoured Field Divisions on the eastern front. It used successfully by the 1st Independent Tank Hunter Company, during the winter battles of February 1943 at river don. One of these vehicles on their way back to Germany was given to the Institute of Military Technology (HTI) for tests and to investigate the technological solutions of the vehicle.

Based on that research, the Ganz factory (one of two big companies, which manufactured the 38M Toldi tanks) made the tank hunter prototype of the Toldi in autumn of 1943 from a 38M Toldi I tank, which was under repair.

The basis of the tank hunter vehicles was a 38M Toldi I. light tank, number plate H-376. This tank produced by GANZ Factory in 1940, served at the 2nd Armoured Cavalry Battalion was knocked out in 1941 in Ukraine. Repaired by GANZ Factory and put back to service in 1942.

The gun, the Pak 40/2 75mm long barrel anti-tank gun came from a Marder II tank hunter, served at the 1st Armoured Field Division at River Don in 1943. Returned to Hungary and tested by the HTI.

It was a very simple up cycling of the 38M Toldi light tank. The turret was removed and an open top and rear crew/fighting compartment was constructed. It was armed with the same gun as the Marder II, the 7,5 cm Pak 40. Strictly speaking the

The tank hunter version of the 38M Toldi parking at the yard of HTI (Hungarian Military Technical Institute) spring of 1944. The vehicle had a borrowed gun from a German Mader tank hunter vehicle for testing. [Sárhidai Gyula]

The very last stopgap upgrade of the 38M Toldi tank was the Hungarian designed anti-tank rocket launcher 44M Buzogány (Mace) system installed on the engine deck, behind the turret. The only known photo was taken by a US sergeant in Bavaria, April-May 1945. [Pálinkás Zsolt]

HTI removed the gun from the Marder II and installed into its home design tank hunter. Its thin armour was only capable to withstand infantry fire and it was designed on an obsolete light tank chassis.

On the top of the engine roof, there was a large, enclosed metal box, that was designed to balance the weight of the bigger, heavier gun and to hold some (not all) of the ammunition. That box extended over the side silhouette, which was a flaw in the design, because it could be more easily been hit by the enemy than for example the ammo storage of the Marder II, which was on the same level as the side of the vehicle. But there was not enough free space for the ammo inside the used Toldi chassis, like on the Pz. Kpfw. II chassis of the Marder II. The box could be turned vertically to access the engine below it.

It was very similar to the Marder II, both in appearance – it was only 140mm narrower and 30mm taller – and in its charactestics, which were nearly the same too. Despite the fact that the troops could find use such vehicle, it never entered mass-production. The main reasons probably were the weak and unreliable torsion bars of the 38M Toldi I, and the Germans were not interested in providing PaK 40 anti-tank guns either. The Hungarian licence production of the PaK 40, 40M 7,5cm anti-tank gun just started in 1944.

The German Pak 40 gun was dismantled from Toldi tank hunter and put back the Marder II which was sent back to Germany. The only proof of this project some photographs taken on the prototype.

The last weapon modification of the 38M Toldi light tank was done in summer of 1944. The Hungarian designed anti-tank rocket launcher 44M Buzogány (Mace) system was installed on the hull, behind the turret.

This project was hidden until recently when a strange photo emerged on the internet. The photo was taken by an US sergeant belonged to the 691st Tank Destroyer Battalion, 3rd US Army, in April-May 1945, somewhere in Bavaria. So far we have no documents about the weapon system, or the installation, neither the location where the photo was taken. On the other hand recently another photo emerged on the installation of the Buzogány (Mace) anti-tank rocket system on 40/43M Zrínyi assault howitzer too.

Technical Data of the 38M Toldi light tanks and its versions

Designation: **38M Toldi I (light tank A20) and Toldi II (light tank B20)**

Years of production: 1939-1940

Factory/produced quantity: Ganz /108, MÁVAG /82

Number plates: Toldi I: H-301-H-381; ToldiII: H-382- H-490

Combat weight: 8,5 t

Length: 4750 mm

Width: 2140 mm
Height: 2020 mm
Ground pressure: 0,5kp /cm/3
Crew: 3
Engine Bussing NAG type L8 V/36 Tr
Displacement: 7913 cm/3
Cylinders: 8
Horsepower: 155 Hp
Max. Speed: 50km/h
Range: 200 km
Obstacle – step: 0,6 m
ditch: 1,75 m
ford: 0,7 m
Armament: one 36M 20mm anti-tank rifle; one 34/37M 8mm machine-gun
Ammunition: 208 x 20mm shell, 52 magazines; 2400 x 8mm rounds 96 magazines
Armour: 5-13mm
Radio: Toldi I R-5 radio with arc antenna; Toldi II R-5/a with stick antenna

Designation: **38M Toldi IIA (light tank B40)**
Years of production: 1942-1944
Factory/ produced quantity: Ganz/ 80
Combat weight: 9,35 t
Length: 4750 mm
Width: 2100 mm
Height: 2020 mm
Ground pressure: 0,547 kp/cm/3
Crew: 3
Engine Bussing NAG Type L8V/36 Tr
Displacement: 7913 cm/3
Cylinders: 8
Horsepower: 155 Hp
Max. Speed: 47 km/h
Range: 190 km
Obstacle – step: 0,60 m
ditch: 1,75 m
ford: 0,70 m
Armament: one 37/42M 40mm L/26 gun; maximum firing range: 8400m;
Rate of fire: 15-16 rounds /minute; one 34/40AM 8mm machinegun
Ammunition: 55 x 40 mm 36M armoured piercing or 39M fragmentation shell; 3200 x 8mm cartridge
Armour: 35-13mm
Radio: R-5/a with stick antenna

Designation: **43. M Toldi IIIA (light tank C40) prototype**
Years of production: 1942-1943
Factory: HTI/Ganz
Number plate: H-483
Combat weight: 9,45 t
Length: 4750 mm
Width: 2140 mm
Height: 2070 mm
Ground pressure: 0,61 kp/cm/3
Crew: 3
Engine Ganz VIII VGT.107
Displacement: 7913 cm/3
Cylinders: 8
Horsepower: 155 Hp
Max. Speed: 45 km/h
Range: 190 km
Obstacle – step: 0,60 m
ditch: 1,75 m
ford: 0,70 m
Armament: one 42M 40mm gun; one 34/40AM 8mm machine-gun
Ammunition: 87 x 36M armoured piercing and 39M fragmentation shell; 3200 x 8mm cartridge
Armour: 35 - 6mm
Radio: R-5/a radio with stick antenna

Designation: Toldi Tank Hunter (prototype)
Years of production: 1943-44
Factory: Ganz, HTI
Combat weight: 10,5 t
Length: 4750 mm
Full length with barrel: 5640 mm

Width: 2140 mm
Height: 2230 mm
Ground pressure: 0,63 kp/cm/3
Crew: 3, Commander/Radioman, Gunner, Driver
Engine Ganz VIII VGT.107
Displacement: 7913 cm/3
Cylinders: 8
Horsepower: 155 Hp
Max. Speed: 45 km/h
Range: 190 km
Obstacle – step: 0,60 m
ditch: 1,75 m
ford: 0,70 m
Armour: 23 – 6mm
Armament: one 7,5cm Pak 40/2 L/46 (40M 75cm anti-tank gun in Hungarian service)
Ammunition: 21 rounds
Planned additional machine gun against infantry and air targets
Radio: no data

Ammunition Rates of the Armoured Forces Vehicles
The following shows the official ammunition carrying capacity of the vehicles:
38. M Toldi I-II: 208 x 20mm and 2400 x 8mm
38. M Toldi IIA: 55 x 40mm and 3200 x 8mm
38. M Toldi III: 87 x 40mm 3200 x 8mm

Vehicle Costs

During production there was an ongoing discussion between the Ministry of Defence and the factories about the prices to be charged for each vehicle. In reality, the price actually paid by the Ministry was a compromise; more or less half-way between the prices asked for by the factories and the offer prices from the Ministry. Note: The exchange rate in 1936 was US$1 = 3.40 Pengő. 190.000 Pengő – 150.000 Pengő.

Official Vehicle Designations

The Hungarian-made armoured vehicles had different designations during their use. There were one or more official designations, and of course the troops used their own common names. The names shown in parentheses were official designations used in the later part of the war.

38M Toldi light tank – 1st order (Toldi A20)
38M Toldi light tank – 2nd order (Toldi B20)
38M Toldi IIA light tank (Toldi B40)
38M Toldi III light tank (Toldi C40)
43M Toldi medical tank (Toldi EU20)

CHAPTER 6

Organisation and Training of the Armoured Troops equipped with 38M Toldi light tanks

As already mentioned in the introduction, the Treaty of Trianon prohibited any kind of armoured vehicle or armoured troops for the Hungarian Army. However, the leadership of the Army recognised the importance of this new branch and equipment and remembered the successes that had been achieved by the use of armoured trains and armoured cars during WWI.

The first real tanks of the Hungarian Army were purchased from the stock of the former German Mackensen Army via Sweden, the 14 LK II tanks arrived on barges along the River Danube.

The first real progress made was the establishment of the Police Training School (RUISK), which became the cadre for the new Hungarian armoured branch. The RUISK had an armoured car section of 2-3 armour-plated trucks with a primitive turret.

At first the armoured unit of the RUISK was expanded to the size of an armoured group, and equipment that had been hidden for years from the eyes of the Allies was now gathered and deployed in military depots.

The order of battle of 1930 contained an armoured group with one armoured car and one light tank company, equipped with eight armoured cars, one radio car and five LK II tanks. Due to its good relationship with the Italian military, the Hungarian Army received five Fiat 3000B light tanks, with the shipping being done in secret. They were assigned to the light tank company.

At the beginning the 38M Toldi light tanks were organised alongside the 35M FIAT Ansaldo tankettes and 39M Csaba armoured cars into reconnaissance and armoured cavalry battalions. The photo was taken in summer of 1941, probably at the 1st Armoured Cavalry Battalion which had nine Toldi light tanks too. [Deák Tamás]

38M Toldi I light tanks on tactical manoeuvre advancing under the smoke screen, even from a great distance the military insignia was a telltale sign for the enemy. [War Correspondent Company]

Tank hunter training for infantry, a sapper preparing a demonstration with blasting charge to immobilise the feared armoured vehicle. Interestingly he armed with a 39M Király sub-machine gun. [Szollár János]

Cadet Officers are on a practical training with the 38M Toldi light tank, on the right corner of the photo the headlamp with its cover plate is visible. [Babucs Zoltán]

Boys of the military grammar school curiously exploring the 38M Toldi light tanks on display. They worn dark blue uniform according to the old K. und K. traditions. [Pálinkás Zsolt]

The turning point for the Hungarian armoured forces was an Italian offer to deliver the new CV-33 Fiat-Ansaldo tankette to Hungary. In June 1934 the Military Technical Institute tested the CV-33 tankette and advised that these should be put into service. The Hungarian Army ordered 150 tankettes from Turin and put them into service as the 35 M Fiat-Ansaldo tankette in 1935.

The first mechanised unit of the Hungarian Army, the Experimental Motorised Group, was established in 1932. The reconnaissance battalion of the 2nd Brigade was the first true armour unit of the Hungarian Army with one – one armoured car, tankette and motorised riflecompany. The strength of the unit was based on the 3rd and 4th Tankette Companies and on the armoured cars of the Experimental Mechanised Group. The cavalry brigades also each received a tankette company.

Later, the armoured units of the cavalry brigades were enlarged to battalion size similar to the armoured battalions of the motorised brigades, consisting of one company each of light tanks (38M Toldi), tankettes (35M Ansaldo) and armoured cars (39M Csaba). The companies had 16 vehicles; three platoons each with 5 armoured vehicles plus the company commander's vehicle.

The Ministry of Defence purchased a new self propelled A/A-AT armoured vehicle, the L-62 (40M Nimród) from Landsverk in 1939. The greatest problem was the lack of medium and heavy tanks. Because of the war, Hungary could not purchase these from Germany and Italy. The only solution was a former Czechoslovakian medium tank, the T-21, which was later produced under licence as the Turán tank.

Tank Battalions

As of December 1940, the Mobile Corps order of battle was re-organised following the delivery of the new armoured vehicles (38M Toldi and 39M Csaba). The new plan also included the 40M Nimród and 40M Turán armoured vehicles, even though they were not yet being produced. One cyclist battalion (9th and 11th) of each motorised rifle brigade was converted into a tank

The officer candidates of the Armoured Class of the Ludovika Military Accademy chatting around a 38M Toldi light tank during a summer exercise in 1942, on the left is cadet István Korbuly. [Virág Ajtony]

Officer candidate István Korbuly hand signalling in the turret of a 38M Toldi II light tank, with the temporary turret number white L25. [Virág Ajtony]

The officer candidates were keen on testing the limits of the armoured vehicles; the 38M Toldi II in full speed crossing a ditch, turret number is L25. [Pálinkás Zsolt]

Another 38M Toldi, L33 stuck in a ditch during the summer manoeuvre of the Armoured Class of the Ludovika Academy, next to the immobilised tank is a dispatch rider on its Puch G350 motorbikes. [Pálinkás Zsolt]

battalion. The tank battalion, theoretically consisting of three light and one medium tank companies, each had 23 tanks plus the battalion staff with three light tanks and one medium tank and two A/A-AT companies, each with six 40M Nimróds. The new, reorganised battalions officially were named as 9th and 11th Cyclist-Tank Battalion. During the transition period the battalions consisted of battalion staff, sapper, signals, maintenance platoons and 2-2 light tank and cyclist companies.

Due to the lack of light tanks, the motorised and cavalry brigades transferred their Toldi companies to the newly created tank battalions, and the cavalry brigades received the tankette companies of the motorised rifle brigades. The armoured cavalry battalions released half of their 38M Toldis. Nine light tanks remained with the battalions to reinforce the 35M Ansaldo companies. These complicated changes resulted in a motorised rifle brigade having one tank battalion and one reconnaissance battalion.

Under the new organisation, the motorised rifle brigades had one light tank battalion and one reconnaissance battalion, and the cavalry brigade had one armoured battalion. The 1st Motorised Rifle Brigade had the 9th Cyclist-Tank Battalion, and the 2nd Brigade had the 11th Cyclist-Tank Battalion. The battalions' title and organisation reflected on the transitional sate of them.

On 20 June 1941 the 9th and 11th Battalions each received 18 Toldi light tanks from the central reserve. The tank battalions had two companies of light tanks; each equipped with 18 Toldi tanks and the replacement/training unit with 8 Toldi tanks.

The cyclist-tank battalions consisted of the battalion HQ (3 Toldi), sapper, signals, maintenance platoons and the 1st, 2nd Cyclist Companies and the 3rd, 4th Tank Companies (18-18 Toldi light tanks). As of 1 July 1941, the 9th Cyclist- Tank Battalion equipment consisted of 39 Toldi light tanks, 52 trucks, 11 cars, 37 solo, 2 sidecar motorbikes, 2 ambulances, 1-1 signal and fuel truck. The cyclist companies had 206 bicycles/company.

Cadre units with 8 Toldi light tanks each remained at home as reserve and replacement for their battalions.

This new organisation was completed immediately prior to Hungary becoming involved in the Barbarossa Campaign. With the start of the campaign in the summer of 1941, the Mobile Corps with its 38M Toldi light tank units was deployed into the Ukraine.

New organisation

The next reorganisation of the armoured forces took place in October 1941, while the Mobile Corps was still fighting in Ukraine. The idea was to form an armoured division, the 2nd with one tank and one motorised rifle brigades. It based on the German armoured division's order of battle. The Mobile Corps was re-organised with the new unit, the 2nd Armoured Division, which was made up of:

2nd Armoured Brigade, (newly created)
2nd Motorised Brigade, (already in existence)
51st A/A-AT Battalion (newly created)

The 1st Motorised Rifle Brigade, (already in existence) was also belonged to the Mobile Corps.

The 2nd Armoured Brigade had four battalions, 1/I, 2/I, 3/I, 4/I, which were organised from the 10th, 12th, 13th, 16th, Cyclist Battalions. The 31st Independent Battalion was organised from the 9th Tank Battalion, while the 32nd Independent Battalion was created from the 11th Tank Battalion.

The officer cadets trying to recover their 38M Toldi light tank, probably the L25 after an unsuccessful obstacle crossing. It happened at Esztergomtábor training field, which was allocated for the Armoured Troops in 1942. [Pálinkás Zsolt]

The officer candidates built a hoist system which would connect with other Toldi light tanks to extract the immobilised 38M Toldi light tank from its captivity. [Pálinkás Zsolt]

The newly created battalions were equipped only with 38M Toldis, since the 40M Turán and 40M Nimród tanks were still in production. The tank battalion had three companies, initially two mediums and one light, later three medium companies. The A/A-AT battalion had three companies of 40M Nimróds.

According to this plan the tank battalions of the rifle brigades (31st and 32nd) remained with the brigades. They have a reduced strength of two light companies (2 x 22 Toldi tanks) and one A/A-AT company (6 Nimród). At the same time, the Hungarian war industry had received an enormous order to produce new armoured vehicles; 38M Toldi, 39M Csaba, 40M Nimród and medium 40M Turán vehicles, plus the new modified heavy 41M Turán tank.

In the meantime armoured units of the Mobile Corps were continuing to fight on the Eastern Front but due to the difficult terrain their casualties were mounting and the damaged vehicles were sent for repair to the factories. This explains why in 1942 the Hungarian Army had in its order of battle only one tank regiment and two independent tank battalions but no real armoured units.

1st Armoured Field Division

In 1942 Hungary sent its 2nd Army to Russia, but due to the lack of Hungarian vehicles its armoured division was equipped with German tanks. The unit was designated the 1st Armoured Field Division and it was an ad hoc formation, not included in the order of battle.

The 38M Toldi tanks for the 1st Armoured Field Division were amassed from the armoured cavalry battalions.

The armoured equipment of the 1st Armoured Field Division comprised of 24 Pz. IVF-1, 108 Skoda 38(t), 14 x 39M Csaba, 18 x 38M Toldi and 19 x 40M Nimród armoured vehicles plus 6 Pz. Befehlwagen command vehicles .

Final organisation

Based on combat experiences during 1941, the General Staff of the Hungarian Army modified the organisation of the Mobile Brach. It became clear that the deployment of different kinds of troops (mechanised, cavalry and cyclist) in one unit was not satisfactory.

Armoured Divisions

In October 1942 the Mobile Corps was converted into the I Armoured Corps consisting of the Corps' HQ, 1st and 2nd Armoured Divisions, and the 1st Armoured Signal Battalion (three signal companies). The organisation of the new armoured divisions consisted of one tank and one motorised rifle regiment, with three battalions of each plus one reconnaissance battalion, one engineer battalion, a signal battalion, an A/A artillery battalion and a A/A-AT battalion, three mechanised artillery battalions, plus supply units.

Six tank battalions were organised into two tank regiments. The battalions had two medium and two heavy companies and one staff and one supply company.

The 1st Armoured Division (newly created) received the 1st Tank Regiment from the 2nd Armoured Brigade (2nd Armoured Division). The Regiment was made up of the 1/I, 2/I, 1/II (31st Independent) Battalions. The 2nd Armoured Division, in existence from October 1941, included the newly created 3rd Tank Regiment with the 3/I, 4/I and 3/II (32nd Independent) Battalions.

On paper, an armoured division was to have the following armoured vehicles:

66 heavy tank 41M Turán
114 medium tank 40M Turán
82 light tank 38M Toldi
42 A/A-AT vehicle 40M Nimród
14 armoured car 39M Csaba

The role and task of the 38M Toldi light tanks were reevaluated due to the lessons learned and organised into light reconnaissance platoons attached to the medium, heavy tank companies as well as to staff companies of the tank battalions and regiments and served as command vehicles at the 40M Nimród Sp. AT-AA units.

The tank regiment consisted of one of each staff, sapper and maintenance company. The staff company had three 40M Turán tanks (2 commander, 1 normal vehicles) plus a reconnaissance platoon with 5 x 38M Toldi light tanks. The battalion staff company had a similar complement with the addition of one Nimród platoon equipped with one 38M Toldi light tank and 4 x 40M Nimród A/A-AT vehicles. The heavy companies were equipped with 11 x 41M heavy Turán tanks plus a reconnaissance platoon with 5 x 38M Toldi tanks. The medium companies had 17 x 40M medium Turán tanks and 5 x 38M Toldi light tanks at the reconnaissance platoon. The tank battalion also had a supply company.

The A/A-AT battalion had one 38M Toldi light tank for the battalion staff, and 6 x 40M Nimróds plus one 38M Toldi tank for each of the three companies. The reconnaissance battalion had one 39M Csaba armoured car for the battalion staff and 13

Armoured reserve officer training course at the 1/II Tank Battalion at the barracks of Jászberény, 1942-1943. Behind the 38M Toldi I tank, inside the garage a Polski FIAT 508 staff car is visible. The stripe on the sleeve of the troopers represented that they are grammar school graduates eligible for reserve officer training. [Babucs Zoltán]

x 39M Csaba armoured cars for the armoured car company. In 1943 the armoured units were located as follows:

1st Armoured Division
1 /I Tank Battalion, Esztergom
1 /II Tank Battalion, Jászberény
1 /III Tank battalion, Rétság
2nd Armoured Division
3/I Tank Battalion, Cegléd
3/II Tank Battalion, Kecskemét
3/III Tank Battalion, Kiskunhalas

1st Cavalry Division

The division included the 1st Cavalry Tank Battalion with one heavy and three medium companies plus the staff company, altogether 25 x 38M Toldis, 54 medium 40M Turáns and 11 heavy 41M Turán tanks. Other sources put the totals at 56 medium, 11 heavy Turáns and 5 light Toldi tanks, plus three 38(t) tanks for training.

Assault training Cadres

The Hungarian Army organised assault gun battalions which it was planned to equip with Hungarian-made Zrínyi assault guns/howitzers. On 1 October 1943, the 1st and the 10th Assault Gun Battalions and the 2nd-8th Assault Gun Training Cadres were formed. These cadres were organised for training crews for the battalions, and in April 1944 these cadres were converted into assault gun battalions. By this time, training had started with Toldi and Turán tanks. The 1st Assault Gun Battalion had 10 x 41M heavy Turán and 10 x 38M Toldi light tanks, and the 2nd,8th Assault Gun Training Cadres received 7 heavy 41M Turán tanks.

Occupational Forces

The 102nd Independent Occupational Armoured Company was organised by the 1/II Tank Battalion in 1943. The Company had two light tank platoon with 3-3 38M Toldi tank and two armoured car platoon with 3-3 39M Csaba armoured car.

38M Toldi light tank at Armoured Training

Officer's education

As of 1934 the Ludovika Military Academy began regular education of young armoured officer candidates. In the first year only four candidates began their training. Later the number of candidates was enlarged. At the same time reserve training for the armoured branch was started. An Armoured Class for professional officers was established at the Ludovika Military Academy in 1940.

The Ludovika Academy released 217 armoured officers from 1938 until 1944. Forty-six of them were killed in action during the war.

The Armoured Class of the Ludovika Academy had three three 35M Ansaldo tankettes, 39M Csaba armoured cars three 40M Turán tanks, ten 38M Toldi light tanks and one 40M Nimród A/A-AT vehicle in 1943-44.

The "Csaba Királyfi" Mobile Troops Cadet School was established at Marosvásárhely, where candidates received four years of military education and one year practical experience with the mobile troops, after which they were promoted to the rank of Ensign. The Cadet School had three Csaba armoured cars in 1943.

NCO training

The professional NCOs were trained at the Kinizsi Pál NCN School at Veszprém/Juttas from 1924 until 1944. The NCO School had one-one infantry, artillery and mobile training battalion. The mobile battalion consisted of one-one cavalry and armoured companies. From 1934, selected enlisted men could apply to the NCO School. The two years long training course was famously thought and demanding. The graduates were respected and feared by the conscripts and valued by the officers. The School had four 39M Csaba armoured cars in 1944.

CHAPTER 7

Operational history of the Armoured Troops equipped with 38M Toldi light tanks

The 38M Toldi light tanks were the backbone of the Hungarian Armoured Forces in the early years of the war, 1940-1941. These light tanks were intensively used during the operation in Transylvania, Yugoslavia and Ukraine in 1941. The Toldi light tanks served in the light tank companies of the reconnaissance, armoured cavalry and bicycle-light tank battalions.

However, operational experiences showed that the 38M Toldi tank was a light tank, dedicated to perform reconnaissance tasks subordinated to medium and heavy tank companies and battalions. Basically the 38M Toldi light tank was a very mobile, but lightly armoured and armed tank.

Based on the request of the Armoured Forces some upgrades were done to make the Toldi light tank more compatible with the enemy armoured vehicles. Half of the tanks were up gunned with 40mm gun already totally outdated to fight the main enemy the Soviet T-34 medium tank. Experimental skirt plates were attached to the tank but it weighted extra 500 kilograms, too much to the engine of the Toldi.

After a short internal organisational period, when the 1st Armoured Field Division was formed and deployed to the Eastern Front the Toldi light tanks were organised into reconnaissance platoons within the medium and heavy tank companies, tank and cavalry tank battalions, and regimental staff of the tank regiments. Single Toldi tanks war used as command vehicles at the Sp. AT-AA battalions and companies too.

Factory fresh 38M Toldi I light tanks belonged to one of the armoured cavalry battalions waiting for the marching orders. Behind the light tanks is the command element of the armoured car company with Mercedes G5 command car, dispatch riders and the 39M Csaba armoured cars. [Szollár János]

Armoured vehicles of the 1st Reconnaissance Battalion at Szászrégen in September 1940. The 38M Toldi I light tanks and 39M Csaba armoured cars wearing the white Maltese cross military insignia developed by the 1st Reconnaissance Battalion. [Fortepan]

One of the armoured cavalry battalion assembled at the town's square in Transylvania, the vehicles has no military insignias, lined after each other the 35M FIAT Ansaldo tankettes, 38M Toldi I light tanks and the 39M Csaba armoured cars. [Mujzer Péter]

The Light Tank Company of the 1st Reconnaissance Battalion advancing trough the Carpathian Mountains, the difficult terrain and roads were an appetiser for the operation in Ukraine next year. [Szollár János]

38M Toldi I light tank belonging to the 1st Reconnaissance Battalion passing the Hungarian native local civilians in a Transylvanian town, September 1940. [Pálinkás Zsolt]

Bivouac of the Light Tank Company of the 1st Reconnaissance Battalion somewhere in Transylvania. The camouflaged tents were made up from two shelters half, for two men, a very cramped space indeed. During the rest the maintenance crew franticly worked on the factory fresh vehicles to keep the moving. [Szollár János]

From the second part of the war, practically from spring of 1944, the 38M Toldi tanks played a secondary, subordinated role in the war fighting. However it was used until the end of the war.

1940 Transylvania

The first operation of the 38M Toldi light tank dated back to the hot September of 1940.

For Hungary the loss of Transylvania, because of its size, population and resources, was the biggest blow resulting from the Trianon Treaty, which had awarded this territory to Romania. This loss was a continuing source of irritation to Hungarians, and its return to Hungary was a vital issue.

The hot summer of 1940 seemed to be perfect for the Hungary to achieve her goal of recovering the lost territory. The Germans were fighting on the Western Front and the Soviet

Light Tank Company of the 1st Reconnaissance Battalion, 38M Toldi I light tank had a small tricolour pennant attached to the searchlight. [Szollár János]

Rear view of the 38M Toldi I light tank column of the Light Tank Company of the 1st Reconnaissance Battalion on the same spot of the road in Transylvania, September 1940. [Szollár János]

Light Tank Company of the 1st Armoured Cavalry Battalion waiting for the marching order in Transylvania. The 38M Toldi I light tanks had no military insignia, came right from the factory. On the right corner of the picture is a Puch G350 motorbike. [Illésfalvy Péter]

38M Toldi I light tanks of a light tank company lined up with their dispatch riders with Puch G350 motorbikes during the Transylvanian operation, September 1940. [Pálinkás Zsolt]

38M Toldi I light tank of the 1st Reconnaissance Battalion passing an arch triumph in a village of Transylvania, September 1940. [Szollár János]

Parading 38M Toldi light tanks passing the grandstand with the dignitaries in front of Admiral Miklós Horthy, governor of Hungary at Kolozsvár, September 1940. [War Correspondent Company]

Light Tank and Armoured Car Companies of the 1st Reconnaissance Battalion, resting on the road in the late summer heat in September 1940. The 38M Toldi I light tanks wearing the white Maltese cross military insignia. [Szollár János]

38M Toldi I light tank and Mercedes G5 command car of the 1st Reconnaissance Battalion and their troops celebrated with the local Hungarian population the return of Transylvania, September 1940. [Szollár jános]

Parading 38M Toldi I light tank passing the celebrating population in a Transylvanian town. The flags with swastika on the buildings clearly shown the sphere of influence. [Szollár jános]

Tank platoon of 38M Toldi I light tanks of the 1st Reconnaissance Battalion entering into a small village in Transylvania, September 1940. [Szollár János]

A group photo taken on the crew of a light tank platoon belonged to the 1st Reconnaissance Battalion, the troopers worn the leather coat without the leather trouser which was uncomfortable and hot in summer time. [Szollár János]

Young reserve officers, troop and tank commanders standing in front of their 38M Toldi I light tank in Transylvania, belonged to the 1st Reconnaissance Battalion. [Szollár jános]

38M Toldi light tank belonged to the Light Tank Company of the 1st Reconnaissance Battalion, September 1940, Transylvania. The three men crew position is well visible on the photo. [Szollár János]

Local Hungarian civilians celebrating the entering 38M Toldi I light tanks of the 1st Reconnaissance Battalion in September 1940. [Szollár János]

Another photo of the celebrating local Hungarian civilians with the 38M Toldi I light tanks of the 1st Reconnaissance Battalion in September 1940. On the left corner of the photo the commander's cupola hatch is visible. [Szollár János]

Embarrassed Hungarian children and happy crew of the 38M Toldi I light tank of the 1st Reconnaissance Battalion on the top of their vehicle, the 34/37AM machine gun is on anti aircraft mounting. [Szollár János]

Celebrating civilians in their best dress climbing on a 38M Toldi I light tank belonged to the 1st Reconnaissance Battalion, September 1940. [Szollár János]

Advancing 38M Toldi I light tanks of the 1st Reconnaissance Battalion negotiate dirt road in Transylvania, September 1940. [Szollár János]

A 38M Toldi I light tank in recovery mode towing a broken down army truck in Transylvania, September 1940. [Szollár János]

Light Tank Company with 38M Toldi I light tanks returned from Transylvania at the barracks, waiting for inspection. [Szollár János]

Light Tank Company resting alongside the road waiting to proceed, the troops suffered from constant traffic jams during the operation in Transylvania, the crew gathering around their 38M Toldi I light tanks. [Szollár János]

Crossing a river in Transylvania, the crew of the 38M Toldi I light tank belonged to the 1st Reconnaissance Battalion watching the troops crossing the river on a military bridge, their 34/37AM machine gun is on anti aircraft mounting. [Szollár János]

Returning troops from Transylvania on rail transportation, the 38M Toldi I light tanks easily fit into a normal flat car, in September 1940. [Szollár János]

The operation had a very strict timeline and the road network was limited, which caused traffic jams and accidents as well as. An accident occurred with a 38M Toldi I light tank of the 1st Reconnaissance Battalion. [Szollár János]

Troops of the 1st Reconnaissance Battalion trying to salvage the 38M Toldi I light tank turned to its side in Transylvania. [Szollár János]

The 38M Toldi I light tank of the 1st Reconnaissance Battalion, not just turned to its side but hit a pylon too. The troops were exhausted; the tanks were new and not tested before, a recipe for accidents. [Szollár János]

Not having recovery vehicles the troops used another 38M Toldi I light tank to recover the unlucky Toldi tank in Transylvania, September 1940. [Szollár János]

Another 38M Toldi arrived to helping the recovery, supervised by a local shepherd in Transylvania, September 1940. [Szollár János]

Union had forwarded an ultimatum to Romania to hand back Bukovina and Bessarabia, which had been occupied by the Romanians following WWI.

To back up their demands, the Hungarians mobilised their armed forces; as of 10 July, three armies were deployed in the south-east part of Hungary. The mobile troops were allocated a vital role in the planned operations against the Romanian forces. The Mobile Corps was formed with two cavalry and two motorised rifle brigades; however these units were incomplete as regards military hardware. The armoured and reconnaissance battalions had received most of their 38M Toldi light tanks and 39. M Csaba armoured cars at the assembly area only at the last minute. The factory-fresh vehicles were incomplete and had a lot of mechanical failures.

The armoured troops were at 2/3 strength, and only forty 38M Toldi tank were with the light tank companies. The troops had received the new 38M Toldi in a piecemeal fashion. The light tanks were not completed, some of the vital instruments, equipments were missing, like the radios, periscopes, not mentioning the spare parts.

The motorised infantry battalions also got the new 38M Botond trucks, which also arrived at the assembly area.

The date for the advance set by the Hungarian Chief of the General Staff, General Henrik Werth was 28 August 1940. At the last minute the Romanians asked for arbitrage by the German and Italian governments, and this was accepted by Hungary. The second Vienna Arbitrage gave back a part (Northern Transylvania) of the disputed territory to Hungary.

The military occupation of Northern Transylvania was carried out from 5 to 13 of September. Almost the entire mobilised army took part, 550,000 men with their equipment and vehicles. Northern Transylvania became a huge, never-ending military traffic jam. Only the troops of the Mobile Corps managed to reach the far borders of the recovered territory.

The poor state of the roads created many mechanical problems for the mobile forces. The majority of the tanks fresh from the factory and the mobilised civilian trucks broke down and had to be withdrawn from service without even having seen any enemy activity.

1941 Yugoslavian Campaign

On 6 April 1941 the German Army attacked Yugoslavia. Hungary was one of the assembly points for the German troops. At the request of the Germans, Hungary prepared her own troops to take part in the campaign. The Yugoslav state began to fall apart, generating a power vacuum and resultant threat to the Hungarian minorities in Yugoslavia, and this was the pretext that Hungary needed to act.

Soon after the beginning of the German attack, an independent Croatia was declared, and the Hungarian 3rd Army (I, IV, V Corps) and the Mobile Corps, with supporting troops, began their attack on 11 April.

The Mobile Corps was comprised of the 1st and 2nd Cavalry and the 1st and 2nd Motorised Rifle Brigades. The mobile troops were in the midst of reorganising the new tank battalions. The armoured cavalry battalions received their two tankette companies, but without the 38M Toldi platoons. Due to the slowness of mobilisation and a lack of armaments, the forces were not at full strength.

The 2nd Motorised Infantry Brigade lacked 10 light tanks and 8 armoured cars, 135 motorcycles and 21 miscellaneous wheeled vehicles.

38M Toldi I light tank belonged to the 2nd Reconnaissance Battalion, wearing the circle shape military insignia and the white 2F unit sign occupied a captured Serbian barrack in Voivodina, April 1941. [Fortepan]

38M Toldi I light tanks advancing trough a village in Voivodina in April 1941, participating in the first real combat operation of the Hungarian Army. [Szollár János]

Local Hungarian civilians fraternising with the armoured troops in a village of Voivodina. The 38M Toldi I light tanks not wearing military insignia just Mechanised Branch Sign. [Mujzer Péter]

38M Toldi I light tank belonged to the Light Tank Company of the 1st Armoured Cavalry Battalion towing a broken 37M Hansa Lloyd half-tracked artillery tractor during the operation in Yugoslavia/ Voivodina in April 1941. [Fortepan]

38M Toldi I light tank passing German horsed artillery unit in Voivodina/Yugoslavia in April 1941. The commander had the 39M crash helmet with earphone. [Jean-Francois Antoina]

Hungarian operations in Yugoslavia in April of 1941

38M Toldi I light tank, number plate H-320, belonged to the 1st Reconnaissance Battalion providing close protection to the HQ of the 1st Motorised Rifle Brigade probably at Újvidék/Novi Sad, the Brigade pennant hung over the main door of the building, April 1941. The light tank already wears the new octagonal military insignia. [Mujzer Péter]

38M Toldi I light tanks of the 2nd Reconnaissance Battalion embarking for rail transport at the end of the operation, the closest Toldi had the number plate H-304 and the circle shape military insignia, drives on the flat car. [Szollár János]

The 1st Armoured Cavalry Battalion was deployed without its anti-tank, signal, engineer and light tank platoons.

The 2nd Armoured Cavalry Battalion's tankette companies had eighteen 35M Ansaldo and three 38M Toldi light tanks.

When the Hungarian forces began their attack, the Serb fortifications were partially abandoned by the regular Serb troops. The Hungarian forces occupied this territory after only minor clashes.

The 1st Armoured Cavalry Battalion (1 company each of armoured cars, light tanks and tankettes) was reinforced with a light howitzer battery. The battalions started their advance on the afternoon of 11 April 1941. The armoured car and light tank companies reached the Serb fortifications, which were abandoned.

The Light Tank Company of the 1st Reconnaissance Battalion came face to face with Serb troops at Zombor (Sombor) on the morning of 12 April 1941. After a short, but heavy fight, the Hungarian 38M Toldi light tanks captured 74 Serb soldiers, 4 anti-tank guns and 6 light machine guns.

On 13 April 1941, one of the tankette companies of the 2nd Armoured Cavalry Battalion was ordered to reconnoitre the Serb bunkers at Szabadka (Subotica). The company commander's Toldi tank hit a mine, but the only damage inflicted was the loss of a track. The Serb defenders left their trenches.

On 13 April, patrols of the 1st Reconnaissance Battalion scouting near Petrőc (Backi Petrovac) came across a withdrawing Serb infantry regiment, armed with 12 anti-tank guns, heading in the direction of Újvidék (Novi Sad). Lieutenant Gyula Keresztes armoured car platoon encountered the Serbian infantry. The majority of the reconnaissance battalion joined to attack the flanks of the Serb infantry at Petrőc (Backi Petrovac) and Dunagálos (Glozan). 1st Lieutenant Ferenc Antalfy commander of the Light Tank Company also came to break the enemy resistance. After a short but intensive Hungarian fusillade, the Serbs capitulated. The Hungarian troops captured 30 officers and 1000 enlisted men, and the battalion reached Újvidék (Novi Sad) at 16.00 hours.

As of 14 April, the motorised brigades of the Mobile Corps were reassigned to the German Panzer Group Kleist, however the campaign came to a swift conclusion and they were assigned the duty of securing the area of Eszék (Osijek) –Vinkovci –Vukovár (Vukovar).

Due to the size of the 38M Toldi I light tank, three could stored on two railway flat cars to make the transportation more economic. The armoured units of the Mobile Corps returned by rail from the operation to preserve the motor vehicles. The new octagonal military insignia and the Mechanised Branch Sign painted on the tank turret. [Szollár János]

Soviet Campaign 1941

When the Germans had begun preparing for the Barbarossa Campaign, they had not intended to involve Hungary as a fighting participant in the war against Russia. When the war broke out between Germany and Russia, the Hungarians closed the Hungarian-Russian border and reinforced the frontier guard units and air defences.

On June 26, 1941 three unidentified twin-engine bombers attacked the Hungarian town of Kassa (Kosice). The following morning Hungarian bombers attacked Russian targets in Ukraine, and Russia and Hungary were at war.

An operational group was formed to carry out the military activity against Russia. It was called the "Carpathian Group", commanded by Lieutenant General Ferenc Szombathelyi, and consisted of the VIII Corps (1st Mountain Brigade and 8th Frontier Guard Brigade) and the Mobile Corps.

The Mobile Corps was led by Major General Béla dálnoki Miklós and comprised of three brigades: the 1st and 2nd Motorised Rifle and 1st Cavalry Brigades. The Mobile Corps was reinforced with the I, V, VIII Artillery Battalions, the VI, VII Bicycle Battalions, and the 152nd Engineer and 150th Signal Battalions.

The Mobile Corps had received its mobilisation order at its peacetime bases on 26 June. It was ordered to assemble ready

Light tank company advancing on the cobblestone road in Galicia July of 1941. Comparing with the roads in Ukraine it was a state of art highway. The 38M Toldi I tanks at the light tank battalions were collected from different units, wearing the previous units' signs like the third and fourth Toldi tanks previously belonged to the 1st Armoured Cavalry Battalion, however the military insignia was the standard octagonal one. [War Correspondent Company]

The heavily camouflage 38M Toldi I tanks and Ford supply trucks of the 9th Bicycle –Light Tank Battalions resting next to an old fort, probably at Kamenyec-Podolski, July of 1941. [Szollár János]

The tanks of the 9th Bicycle –Light Tank Battalion are carefully camouflaged with green branches parking alongside of a Polish mansion house in Eastern Galicia July of 1941. [Szollár János]

Crossing the Carpathian Mountains on track was already a challenging task for the mechanised troops, a light tank company advancing trough a mountain road.

The supply tail of the tank battalions consisted of some 38M Botond all terrain trucks, but mainly based on the Ford and Ford-Marmon trucks with limited cross country capability. [Szollár János]

The Soviet troops resisted fiercely in the build up areas, which caused a significant damages, 38M Toldi I light tank advancing trough the ruins of Kolomea. [War Correspondent Company]

Position of the Mobile Corps troops from 27 to 31 of July 1941

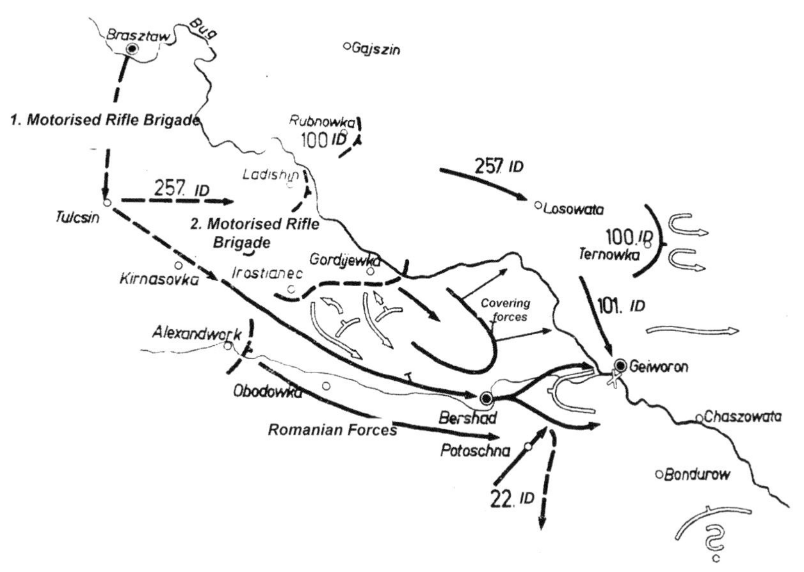

German dispatch rider stand with the Hungarian armoured troopers covered in dust in Galicia July 1941, the Hungarians probably belonged to the 9th Bicycle – Light Tank Battalion cooperating with the German jagers of the 101st German Light Infantry (Jager) Division. [Jean-Francois Antoina]

for marching forward by 29 June. Mobilisation was very slow and was not completed. At the time of moving out, its strength was only about 75-80%.

Under the new organisation, the motorised rifle brigades had one light tank battalion and one reconnaissance battalion, and the cavalry brigade had one armoured battalion. The 1st Motorised Rifle Brigade had the 9th Bicycle-Tank Battalion, and the 2nd Brigade had the 11th Bicycle-Tank Battalion. The battalions' title and organisation reflected on the transitional sate of them.

Colonel Vilmos Néray commanded the 9th Bicycle-Tank Battalion. Captain Tibor Kárpáthy commanded the 3rd Light Tank Company of the 9th Bicycle-Tank Battalion. The 4th Company was led by Major Ferenc Demitrovits .

Colonel József Heinz was the commander of 11th Bicycle-Tank Battalion and later he commanded the Field Tank Battalion which was organised from the serviceable tanks of the 9th and 11th Battalions. Captain Géza Mészöly was the company commander of the 3rd Light Tank Company, 11th Bicycle-Light Tank Battalion.

The bicycle-tank battalions consisted of the battalion HQ (3 x 38M Toldi light tanks), sapper, signals, maintenance platoons and the 1st and 2nd Bicycle Companies and 3rd and 4th Tank Companies (18-18 x 38M Toldi light tanks).

As of 1 July 1941, the 9th Bicycle- Tank Battalion equipment consisted of 39 x 38M Toldi light tanks, 52 trucks, 11 cars, 37 solo, 2 sidecar motorbikes, 2 ambulances, 1-1 signal and fuel truck. The bicycle companies had 206 bicycles/ company.

Cadre units, with 8 x 38M Toldi light tanks each remained at home as reserve and replacement for their battalions.

The 1st Cavalry Armoured Battalion had one armoured car company and two tankette companies (9 x 38M Toldi light tanks and 36 x 35M FIAT Ansaldo tankettes). Each tankette company had three tankette platoons (6 x 35M Ansaldo tankettes each), and one light tank platoon (4 x 38M Toldi light tank). The remaining one 38M Toldi light tank was with the battalion staff.

Colonel Ferenc Révhegyi commanded the 1st Armoured Cavalry Battalion during the operation in Ukraine, on 21 August

38M Toldi I light tank probably belonged to the 3rd Light Tank Company of the 9th Bicycle – Light Tank Battalion towing a broken down German trucks in July 1941. The Toldi I had no weapons in the turret and used as a recovery vehicle. [War Correspondent Company]

The same 38M Toldi light tank from a different perspective, the position of the military insignia is well visible on the turret, engine deck and on the rear of the vehicle with the white basis of the number plate. [War Correspondent Company]

Lieutenant Colonel László Bercsényi took over the command of the depleted 1st Armoured Cavalry Battalion from Colonel Ferenc Révhegyi.

The Mobile Corps was equipped with 508 light machine guns, 168 machine guns, 52 anti-tank rifles, 12 mortars, 80 anti-tank guns, 60 A/A guns, and 90 field guns. An Air Force group supported the ground troops with 24 fighters, 12 bombers and 36 reconnaissance planes. The armoured elements of the Mobile Corps had 81-87 x 38M Toldi light tanks, 48 x 39. M Csaba armoured cars and 60 x 35M FIAT Ansaldo tankettes.

Damaged 38M Toldi I light tanks collected for repair behind the front line in Ukraine, the maintenance units were over stretched lacking of spare parts, recovery and towing capacity, nevertheless they did everything to keep fighting the armoured units. [Mujzer Péter]

38M Toldi I light tank, number plate H-320 waits for repair, his left side track system with wheels removed, it probably hit a land mine. The weapons are still in the turret probably means the Toldi light tank is in repairable condition. [Szollár János]

Rail transportation of the 9th Bicycle – Light Tank Battalion, behind the 38M Toldi light tank is a 31M light machine gun on 38M tripod. [Babucs Zoltán]

38M Toldi I light tank drive through a Polish village, the road covered with mud due to the heavy rains. The tank still had an old unit sign; white tank silhouette belonged to the 2nd Reconnaissance Battalion. [Szollár János]

38M Toldi I light tank, number plate H-320 from a different angel, the explosion damaged the drive sprocket and the fender too. [Szollár János]

38M Toldi I light tank advancing through an Ukrainians village in early August of 1941, the crew in a relaxed mood wearing field caps instead of crash helmets. The tank still has the white tank silhouette unit sign. [Fortepan]

Tank column passing a village in Ukraine, the first 38M Toldi I light tank number plate is H-356, wearing a smaller than normal military insignia. The armoured cover of the searchlight is in open position. [Fortepan]

Axis troops advancing on the highway pursuing the withdrawing Soviet troops. The Hungarian cavalry and horse drawn supply wagons of the 1st Cavalry Brigade moving alongside the road, the trucks and the Toldi light tank company moving on the road, the closest 38M Toldi I light tank number plate is H-324. [War Correspondent Company]

The "Carpathian Group" began its advance on 30 June, through very difficult mountainous terrain. The withdrawing Red Army created obstacles for the advancing Hungarian troops by blowing up bridges wherever it could. Within the Carpathian Mountains, Russian engineers destroyed 21 bridges, and the rivers in flood also complicated the operations.

During the advance the staff of the Mobile Corps invented a method to chase the withdrawing Russian troops. The two motorised brigades were deployed on different, parallel roads and the cavalry brigade was deployed between them. The forward echelon of a motorised brigade consisted of the reconnaissance battalion, which was reinforced by light tank, A/A gun (40mm 36M Bofors), sapper and traffic control platoons, an artillery battery and a rifle company. The second echelon consisted of one motorised rifle battalion. The third echelon was the main bulk of the brigade. The last one was the rear guard.

The intent in case of contact was to outflank the enemy or hit them from the front. Of course this was the theory; however the reality was normally more complicated. The withdrawing Russian troops showed courage, determination, good fighting skills and carried out many ambushes and counterattacks. Due to the inadequate road network, logistical support for the advancing

38M Toldi I light tank wading through a creek at Makirowka, in August of 1941. The tank had the octagonal military insignia and the Mechanised Branch Sign decals on the turret. [War Correspondent Company]

Mine damaged 38M Toldi I light tank, number plate H-332 checking by Hungarian infantry, still wearing the old white lightning bolt unit sign of the 1st Reconnaissance Battalion. The weapons removed; probably the tank was left behind after a clash with Soviet rearguards. [Szollár János]

troops was difficult; sometimes fuel and ammunition had to be transported to the mobile troops by aircraft. The troops lacked of recovery vehicles and trailers. The maintenance background of the troops was also weak, and the mobilised civilian trucks were in bad condition. Only the 38M Botond trucks could handle the difficult terrain.

The armoured vehicles were sometimes deployed incorrectly, contrary to normal procedures, which caused greater casualties than otherwise may have been incurred. The commanding officers were in real war in first time with equipment and rules of engagement never tested before. They were not aware of the real advantages or disadvantages of the armoured and mobile units and their equipments. Sometimes the commanders issued orders which led to suicide actions.

The 3rd Company of the 9th Bicycle-Tank Battalion (1st Motorised Brigade) was deployed in the vanguard at Nowa Uszica on 13 July to support the break-through of the German 101st Infantry Division. The company, led by Captain Tibor Kárpáthy, was involved in heavy fighting on the road between Antonovka and Filjanovka.

A Russian anti-tank gun from a distance of 200-300 meters knocked out the company commander's 38M Toldi tank. The driver and the gunner were killed, Captain Kárpáthy seriously injured. The 38M Toldi lay helplessly waiting for the next, deadly shot. At that moment, another 38M Toldi commanded by Officer Candidate Sergeant Pál Habel rushed in and stopped between the enemy and the damaged Toldi, protecting the company commander. The next shot hit this brave light tank and all of its crew was perished. The injured company commander was rescued. The 3rd Light Tank Company suffered 60% causalities, six 38M Toldi was knocked out and nine crewmen were killed. The number plates of the knocked out 38M Toldis were: H-306,-314,-315,-316,-397,-399.

The 1st Motorised Rifle and the 1st Cavalry Brigades were requested by the Germans to break through the Stalin Line. The terrain was very difficult, with swamps, crossed by rivers. The

38M Toldi I light tanks, German infantry and supply wagons are somewhere in Ukraine, summer of 1941. The first tank number plate is H-392, the military insignia at the front plate masked by mud to avoid the aiming point for the Soviet anti-tank gunners. [Jean-Francois Antoina]

Advancing 38M Toldi I light tank with large size military insignia and white tank silhouette unit sign. The crew wearing the Italian style padded leather crash helmets. [Pálinkás Zsolt]

38M Toldi I light tank, number plate H-324 probably belonged to the 9th Bicycle-Light Tank Battalion, but still wearing the old lightning bolt unit sign. The 34/37M Gebauer machine gun is on anti aircraft mounting. [Szollár János]

The H-380 Toldi light tank belonged to the 1st Armoured Cavalry Battalion, one-one platoon of 4 light tanks supported the outdated FIAT Ansaldo tankettes. The crew wearing the cotton mechanic overalls instead of the leather protective gear. Behind the tank is a Ford-Marmon truck. [Szollár János]

1st Motorised Rifle Brigade launched its attack from Dunajec and broke through the fortified line at Bar on July 19.

The 1st Motorised Rifle Brigade knocked out 21 Russian tanks, 16 armoured cars, and 12 guns from 19 to 22 July. The Hungarian casualties amounted to 26 killed, 50 wounded, and 10 missing soldiers, with 15 armoured vehicles damaged. Seven 38M Toldi light tank out of a dozen were repairable.

Hungarian 38M Toldi I light tank towing a broken down German truck, which is a French made Renault AGR truck captured by the German Army in France in 1940 and pressed into the Wermacht to improve the mobility. Two Hungarian made 38M Botond all terrain trucks are also on the picture, the only capable trucks to negotiate the muddy terrain after rain. [Szollár János]

After completing the operations and returning the troops of the Mobile Corps held a victory parade in Budapest on 14 December 1941. The parading armoured units were supplement with armoured vehicles from the home based units and depots due to the significant material losses. The 38M Toldi I light tanks drive on the Andrássy Boulevard, the tank on the right side is H-412 and had a small white triangle unit sign painted next to the number plate. [War Correspondent Company]

The 2nd Motorised Rifle Brigade attacked in the direction of Tulchin on July 24. The defending Soviet troops were reinforced and a regimental size unit of the Soviet 96th Mountain Division launched a series of counter-attacks against the Hungarians from Danidovka. The units of the brigade lay in the deep mud along the road at Gordievka. The right flank of the Brigade was held by the 3rd Regiment of the 8th Romanian Cavalry Brigade, which withdrew after the first Russian attack. The 2nd Brigade found itself in danger. The brigade commander re-deployed his tank battalion on the right flank of the Brigade, to replace the missing Romanians.

The commander of the Mobile Corps ordered the 1st Motorised Rifle Brigade, the 11th Bicycle-Tank and the 1st Armoured Cavalry Battalions to turn back and support the units of the 2nd Brigade. The 1st Motorised Rifle Brigade reached the area only with great difficulties. Because of the mud, the troops had to collect horses and cows to tow the armoured and wheeled vehicles.

The 1st Motorised Rifle Brigade arrived at night on July 27 and immediately flanked the enemy. After heavy fighting, the western bank of the River Bug was cleared of the enemy on July 29. However the Hungarian counter-attack was not coordinated, and was not supported by artillery, with the result that the troops suffered heavy causalities.

Colonel Révhegyi led two tankette companies of his 1st Armoured Cavalry Battalion in the direction of Budy to halt the attacking Russian troops on 27 of July. One of the tankette company of the 1st Armoured Cavalry Battalion was almost entirely destroyed.

During this action, according to some memories the commander of attacking Ansaldos reported to the battalion com-

Damaged but recovered 38M Toldi I light tanks of the 9th Tank Battalion covered with snow waiting for repair at the barrack's yard of Jászberény in December 1941. [Babucs Zoltán]

mander that the terrain is not suitable for attack, but he was challenged by Colonel Révhegyi as a coward. He replied back: *"Order confirmed we are going to die"*

Almost all of the attacking FIAT Ansaldos were destroyed, crew were massacred by enemy artillery and infantry fire. It ended the operational carrier of the tankettes in the Hungarian Army.

At the battle of Gordievka on July 27, the casualty rate of the armoured troops was at its highest. During the campaign, eight armoured officers were killed, with five of them falling at Gordievka.

1st Lieutenant vitéz Ferenc Antalffy served at the 11th Bicycle-Light Tank Battalion as company commander of the 2nd Company, his Battalion was tasked to attack the Soviet troops at the south part of Gordievka. The advancing Hungarian light tank companies eliminated the enemy resistance without casualties. The Antalffy Company continued its advance and destroyed an enemy battery and infantry forces. However, they came under the fire of a concealed enemy battery on a difficult terrain. 1st Lieutenant Antalffy's light tank was immobilised. He left his Toldi light tank and fought a hand to hand battle with his service pistol against the overwhelming enemy forces. He was shot and killed. Posthumously he was decorated with the Hungarian Knight Cross with swords.

Lieutenant András Szotyory tank platoon also came under heavy enemy artillery fire. Four Toldi light tank was immobilised by artillery fire. Lieutenant Szotyory ordered its crews to fall back. Meanwhile he led his 38M Toldi tank to flank the Soviet artillery. However his tank was knocked out, his crew were killed. He jumped out with his 9mm service pistol in his hand and killed by enemy fire. Posthumously he was decorated with the Hungarian Knight Cross with swords.

1st Lieutenant Alfréd Szőke also killed in action at Gordijevka as the officer of the 11th Bicycle-Tank Battalion. Posthumously he was decorated with the Hungarian Knight Cross with swords. 11th Lieutenant Géza Rovázy was a platoon commander at the 11th Bicycle-Tank Battalion and wounded in action at Gordievka too.

The tank battalions lost 19 Toldi light tanks during this fight; most of the tanks were repaired and put back to service.

To compensate for the losses, 14 x 38M Toldi, 9 x 39M Csaba and 5 x 35M Ansaldos were sent to the front by rail on July 27. However, due to heavy German rail traffic, the vehicles only arrived at Krivoj-Rog on October 7.

As of 1 August, the Mobile Corps was lacking 320 motorcycles, 56 cars, 147 trucks, 20 tractors, 8 armoured cars and 7 light tanks. On 5 August the strength of the armoured forces was: 43 serviceable 38M Toldi with the troops plus 14 on flat cars, 14 at the field repair shops and 24 totally destroyed or non repairable.

From 10-11 August, the troops of the Mobile Corps were deployed at Konstantinovka- Vosniesiensk, where they came under heavy air raids. The Corps lost 14 soldiers killed and 12 armoured cars, 2 light tanks and 10 trucks were damaged. Hungarian Air Force fighters shot down 8 Russian fighters and 4 bombers for the loss of one Hungarian aircraft.

The mobile troops were allowed a brief period of rest between 17-27 August, to recuperate following the long advance. On September 1, the Corps was reassigned to defend the River Dnieper, south of Dnepropetrovsk. The Hungarians were given a front 200 kilometres long, but they were too weak to set up a rigid defence. The commander of the Corps organised a light defence with bicycle, cavalry and infantry troops along the river and the motorised and armoured troops in mobile reserve.

The 2nd Motorised Rifle Brigade was assigned to a 55 kilometre long defence line, which included the island of Zaporozhets. The 1st Motorised Rifle Brigade had a 100 km long line. The Ankay-Anesini Group (2 bicycle and 2 motorised rifle battalions, 1 armoured battalion and an artillery battalion) were assigned to a 45 kilometre long defence line. Two cavalry battalions (mounted) were kept in reserve, but the rest of the cavalry troops were dismounted and dispersed among the rifle units along the riverbank. On September 5, a strong force of Russian troops attacked the 2nd Motorised Rifle Brigade at Zaporozhets, forcing the exhausted riflemen to withdraw from the island.

From 27 September to 11 October, the Mobile Corps received a respite from the fighting in order to reorganise and recover, in an area south of Tomakovka. On October 10 the cavalry components of the Cavalry Brigade were sent home. In September each light tank battalion had only one company of 38M Toldi tanks. The troops had 35-40 armoured vehicles, which were organised into one Armoured Field battalion based around the 1st Armoured Cavalry Battalion, with the unit sign of the white tulip and triangle.

Review of the 30th Tank Regiment before the deployment to the Eastern Front in April 1942. On the extreme left is a 38M Toldi light tank visible, it was deployed as a medical vehicle. On the right side of the picture are the German training officers. [War Correspondent Company]

At Esztergomtábor Armoured Camp, Air Force reserve 1st Lieutenant István Horthy inspect the armoured vehicles of the 1st Armoured Field Division. He was the son of Admiral Horthy, governor of Hungary. His figure is framed by the anti-tank riffle's barrel and the driver's cupola of the 38M Toldi light tank. [War Correspondent Company]

The units of the motorised rifle brigades were organised into different combat groups. These groups were based on the various motorised rifle battalions, reinforced with engineer, artillery, and A/A troops. The 1st Motorised Rifle Brigade had three combat groups and two reconnaissance subgroups. Necessity dictated that the Toldi light tanks are shared among the combat and reconnaissance groups. Although the light tanks were useless against well-organised and concentrated anti-tank fire, they were very quick and therefore useful as a surprise element during battle. At the 1st Motorised Rifle Brigade, 10-10 x 38M Toldi tanks were assigned to each of two combat groups, while 5 light tanks were assigned to one of the reconnaissance subgroups.

Beginning October 17, the remaining troops advanced towards Isium. The combat groups of the 1st Motorised Rifle Brigade, after heavy fighting, penetrated Mecsebelovka. The defending Russian troops counter-attacked, but the commander of the Brigade deployed his light tanks in a successful action against the Russian infantry.

During this fighting Lieutenant Győző Laczkó killed in action on 20 October. He was sent to the front as replacement in August 1941, to take over the platoon commander position at the 4th Company 9th Bicycle-Tank Battalion. Later he was platoon commander at the 1st Armoured Cavalry battalion fighting at Mecsebelovka, when his Toldi tank's turret was shot at close range by a Soviet anti-tank gun. He was posthumously he was promoted to 1st Lieutenant and decorated with the Hungarian Knight Cross with swords.

The Hungarian forces reached the River Donets at Isium -South on 28-29 October.

The Mobile Corps ceased combat on 6 November and returned to Hungary. During the four months of operations, the Corps covered 2000 kilometres. The overall causalities came

38M Toldi and 40M Nimród armoured vehicles and a Ford-Marmon truck belonged to the 51st Sp. AT-AA Battalion parking in front of the Zichy Casttle at Zsámbék, before the deployment to the front in 1942. [Fortepan]

The 38M Toldi and 40M Nimród armoured vehicles of the 51st Sp. AT-AA Battalion is lined up for flag consecration at the miner town of Dorog. The 38M Toldi I light tank was used as command vehicles at the battalion. [Fortepan]

to 10% of the men and 100% of the 35M Ansaldo, 90% of the 39M Csaba armoured car and 80 % of the 38M Toldis. Out of 95 Toldi tanks, 62 were sent to the factory for repair, while 25 were destroyed. 1200 trucks and 28 guns were also lost during the campaign. In terms of manpower, 855 men were killed, 2845 wounded or missing, and 830 were unavailable due to illness.

1st Armoured Field Division on the Eastern Front 1942/43

In 1942 the Germans had changed their mind about the role of the Hungarian forces in the war. They needed as many troops from foreign allies as they could to send to the front instead of German forces. Germany now forwarded the bill for the support that it had given to Hungary in her claim for compensation for the territorial losses imposed by the Treaty of Trianon. The German demand was for almost the entire Hungarian Army. After long and not too friendly negotiations the Hungarians offered Germany's Chief of the High Command, Field Marshal Keitel, a complete field army, the 2nd Hungarian Army.

The 2nd Hungarian Army had three infantry corps with nine light divisions (each with two infantry and one artillery regiment) and one armoured division and a regiment-sized aviation group, plus supporting units, a total of 250,000 men. The division was designated the 1st Armoured Field Division. It was an

Vehicles of the 51st Sp. AT-AA Battalion on a pre-deployment training in 1942, 38M Toldi light tank, 40M Nimród Sp. AT-AA vehicles, Poski FIAT 508 command car and a Puch G350 motorbike with a happy village boy dressed up as an armoured trooper. That time the ex-Polish vehicles were extensively used by the Hungarian Army. [Fortepan]

Battalion Staff of the 30/II Tank Battalion crossing a shallow river toward the front line, behind the Skoda 38(t) is a 38M Toldi light tank used as an armoured medical vehicle. The Ford-Marmon and Opel Blitz supply trucks visible behind the tanks. [Móker József]

The Regimental First Aid Post of the 30th Tank Regiment had a few Sd.Kfz.250 half-tracked medical evacuation vehicles as well as two 38M Toldi medical tank. The Hungarian made vehicles were painted to panzer grey on the front, not wearing military insignia just the Mechanised Branch Sign. [Pálinkás Zsolt]

38M Toldi light tank and damaged Skoda 38(t) tanks of the 30/I Tank Battalion. The 38M Toldi tank had the white rhombus with mace unit sign of the 30th Tank Regiment. [Bonhardt Attila]

The turret number 222 of the damaged Skoda 38(t) tank belonged to the 2nd Company of the 30/I Tank Battalion. The Skoda tanks were hit by mines and the explosion demolished their track and gear systems. [Bonhardt Attila]

ad hoc unit, organised from different active mobile units which provided the manpower and equipment except the tanks.

On 8 April 1942, the tank regiment, named 30th Tank Regiment of a the 1st Armoured Field Division was formed.

The strength of the division was 12,500 men equipped with 185 armoured vehicles, 453 motorcycles, 325 cars, 1491 trucks and 106 special vehicles (tankers, field ambulances). The division had 24 anti-tank guns(36M 37 and PAK 50, 50mm), 22 light howitzers (37M 105mm), 8 A/A guns (29M 80mm), 4 Bofors guns (36M 40mm)12 medium and 20 light mortars (36M 81mm and 39M 50mm), 28 anti-tank rifles (36M 20mm), 58 machine guns (07/31M Schwarzlose), and 140 light machine guns (31M Solothurn).

However, that time the 38M Toldi light tanks played an insignificant role in number and task too.

The division had a Tank Regiment, the 30th with only two battalions since there were not enough tanks for a third one. The regimental staff had 3 Skoda 38(t), 2 Toldi tanks and 6 Pz. Befehlwagen command vehicles.

The battalions had 52 Skoda 38(t), 11 Pz. IV.F-1 tanks and three 38M Toldi tank. Two Toldis serving at the battalions were converted as medical vehicles. The regiment had a total of 104 Skoda 38(t), 22 Pz. IV.F-1 and 6-6 38M Toldi and Pz.I tanks.

The 51st Sp.A/A-AT Battalion had three companies with six 40M Nimród and one 38M Toldi command tanks each and three 38M Toldi tanks and one 40M Nimrod for the battalion staff.

The Signals Battalion had four 38M Toldi light tank. The armoured equipment of the 1st Armoured Field Division comprised of 24x Pz. IVF-1, 108 x Skoda 38(t) tanks, 14 x 39M Csaba armoured cars, 18 x 38M Toldi light tanks and 19 x 40M Nimród SP AT-A/A vehicles plus 6 Pz. Befehlwagen command vehicles. The Division also got a few Sdkfz. 250. half-tracked medical evacuation vehicles.

The units of the Division were transported by rail to Russia and after the disembarkation the troops reached the operations area from 2 to 6 of July.

The Hungarian 2nd Army was assigned to support the left wing of the German advance to destroy the Red Army at Stalingrad. It was subordinated to the German Army Group B together with the 6th German and 8th Italian Armies.

The main goal of the Hungarian forces was to overcome the Red Army units and reach the River Don in order to establish a defence line along the river. The Hungarians had to hold a line that exceeded 200 kilometres in length, even though they did not have enough forces or equipment to perform their allowed task properly. The III Army Corps was the first unit of the 2nd Army that was deployed against the Russian troops. From June 30 the Hungarian troops were involved in fighting around Tim, a stronghold of the Red Army.

The 2nd Army units advanced and reached the River Don, but several Soviet bridgeheads of varying sizes remained on the Hungarian side of the river, posing a danger to the Hungarian defence. The commander of the 2nd Army, Colonel-General Gusztáv Jány, decided to mop up these bridgeheads with the support of the Armoured Division.

The 1st Armoured Field Division's first task was to support the 7th Light Infantry Division during the attack against the bridgehead at Uryv on 18 July.

However, the Russian forces carried out a night raid against the Hungarian infantry and re-established the bridgehead. Efforts by Hungarian troops to destroy it proved futile, and the unit of the 1st Armoured Field Division was withdrawn on July 20.

The Russian forces now poured reinforcements into the Korotoyak and Uryv bridgeheads. This created a very dangerous situation for the Hungarian defenders, and a new operation was planned to annihilate these bridgeheads. The commander of the 1st Armoured Field Division organised two battle groups plus reserves to carry out the operation. Each group had one tank, one motorised rifle and one artillery battalion. They were equipped with 103 x 38(t), 20 x Pz. IVF-1, 12 x 40M Nimród, 7 x 38M Toldi tanks and 7 x Pak 97/38 75mm anti-tank guns.

The operation began on 7 August, and the advancing Hungarian armoured and infantry units quickly came under heavy Russian air and artillery fire. At Korotoyak the tanks reached the river but could not mop up the bridgehead. Next day, after some reorganisation, the tanks were used as assault guns. They supported the advancing infantry units, and destroyed the enemy strongholds as directed by the infantry. This proved to be a successful tactic and the advancing troops cleared part of the bridgehead on August 9.

The armoured division suffered 387 dead and lost 38 Skoda 38(t), 2 Toldi and 2 Pz. IV tanks were knocked out, although some of them were repairable.

On 13-14 August the 1st Armoured Field Division renewed its attacks against Korotoyak. At that time the strength of the division was depleted to 44 Skoda 38(t), 4 Pz. IVF-1, and five 38M Toldi tanks. The casualties of the division totalled 99 officers, 1632 enlisted men, and the Russians captured 15 Skoda 38(t) tanks from 7 to 18 of August.

After the bridgehead battles ended, the 1st Armoured Field Division was subordinated to Group Cramer, which constituted the only reserve of Amy Group B, on 2 January 1943. At that time the division had 8 short and 8 long-barrelled Pz. IV., 41 Skoda 38(t), two 38M Toldi, 5 Marders self-propelled tank-hunter vehicles, some 40M Nimród, plus 9 Pz. III with German crews.

The Red Army broke through the Hungarian defences at 12-14 of January. After bitter fighting, the Russian forces enveloped and destroyed the outnumbered Hungarian units.

The 1st Armoured Field Division was directly subordinated to the Germans and without their permission it was not allowed to be used for counter-attacks.

On 17 January the 1st Armoured Field Division counter-attacked with four Pz.IV and eight Pz.III tanks towards Dolschik-Ostrogosshk. The attacking Hungarian tanks destroyed a Soviet motorised column, but were recalled by General Cramer.

On 18 January the Division was ordered to seal the gaps, but it was too late and its strength was too weak. The cold weather and the deep snow also created major obstacles for the Hungarian operations.

The 1st Armoured Field Division suffered heavy casualties during the winter battles, losing almost all its armour due to the deep snow, lack of fuel and enemy action. The division had only around 316 officers, 7428 NCO and enlisted men, 500 vehicles and 13 guns in March 1943. About ten armoured vehicles survived the battles. Nine Skoda 38(t), one Pz.IV and two Marders, a few Csaba and Nimród armoured vehicles were transported back to Hungary.

The technical losses of the 1st Armoured Field Division was 107 tanks (22 x Pz.IV, 10 x Pz.III, 64 x Skoda 38(t), 11 x 38M Toldi light tank)

Contrary to the myths, after the war, the 2nd Hungarian Army suffered heavy but not fatal personal casualties on the River Don. During the one year long constant battles 127.000 – 128.000 men were listed as casualties. About 50.000 – 50.000 were killed and wounded and 28.000 were captured by the Red Army. On the other hand the 80% of the army's equipment was destroyed. The material lost on the Eastern Front represented the half of the total equipment of the whole army.

Occupation Forces

From the autumn of 1941 until 1944, Hungarian troops organised into lightly armed brigades, light divisions were also used to secure the rear areas of troops fighting in Ukraine. These Hungarian units were responsible for the defence of railroads, communication and supply networks, however they had difficulties in handling the well-armed Soviet partisans in the region.

To support the 101st and 102nd Occupation Armoured Companies were raised from 1942 to 1944.

The 101st Armoured Company was equipped with French tanks, but the 102nd Armoured Company had 38M Toldi light tanks too.

102nd Independent Armoured Company

The 102nd Independent Armoured was organised by the 1/II Tank Battalion in 1943. The Company had two light tank platoon with three-three 38M Toldi light tank and two armoured car platoon with three-three 39M Csaba armoured car. The Company was commanded by Major Zoltán Parázsó. The task of the Company was to provide a mobile reserve for the Occupation Force East.

The unit was deployed in December 1943 to Kremenyec, later moved to Stanislau.

On 28 of March one - one 39M Csaba armoured car and 38M Toldi light tank were deployed around Kolomea for reconnaissance. They come under enemy fire, 1st Lieutenant Miklós Koós, who sat in the turret of his Csaba armoured car was seriously wounded. The reconnaissance team withdraw.

The Toldi light tank platoon commanded by 1st Lieutenant József Basó was deployed to Lanczin and subordinated to the 44th Hungarian Infantry Regiment. The Regiment commander tasked the light tank platoon to carry out reconnaissance in the area of Kolomea.

On 29 March the three 38M Toldi of the platoon was deployed. According to 1st Lieutenant Basó memories: "*.. we started at early morning from the village towards Kolomea on the road, in peace time fashion with open hatches, tank commanders standing in the open turrets. We were informed that the next village, Sadzawka is still in friendly hands. (...) As soon we left our village we were under enemy gun fire. We drove towards the morning sun, so our vision was blocked. My tank was hit; the enemy shot destroyed the right chain drive and the tank become immobile. I ordered my crew to leave the tank and I jumped out. My driver and gunner followed me. The two other tanks behind me turned right among the houses, but stuck in the wet gardens. Their crews abandoned the tanks because further shots were fired by the enemy. My abandoned tank's turret was also hit and we heard the closing enemy T-34s.*"

The other two Toldi light tank were stuck in the mud when they tried to turn back. 1st Lieutenant Basó pulled together his men and retreated on foot towards the friendly forces. During his retreat he collected dispersed and lost soldiers Hungarians and Germans as well as and led them to the safety.

The Soviet T-34 company continue its advance towards Delatyn. This incident highlighted, that even in the fourth year

38M Toldi I light tank of the 102nd Independent Occupation Armoured company, the tank was painted dark olive green with late style military insignia. The armoured trooper wearing crash helmet and woollen sleeves leather jerkin armed with German MP-40 sub-machine gun. [Karai Sándor]

of the war reconnaissance were carried out without covering infantry, dispatch riders, and the officers were still in a peace time mood or carless.

The abandoned 38M Toldi light tanks were recovered by the Hungarian forces and repaired and put back in service.

The 102nd Company was disbanded upon the deployment of the 2nd Armoured Division to Galicia in April of 1944.

The officers and men were posted to the 3rd Tank Regiment. 1st Lieutenant Basó served at the 5th Heavy Company 3/II Tank Battalion as a platoon commander.

The 2nd Armoured Division in Galicia, 1944

Following the disaster at Stalingrad in February 1943, the Hungarians began to reassess their alliance with Germany and began looking for an opportunity to leave the Axis. The German reaction to this was to occupy Hungary by force on March 19, 1944 and to replace the government (and the Army High Command) with pro-German elements.

After this date German influence was more direct, and the military and government establishments had to follow the German demands and orders. Already in the autumn of 1940, the Hungarian General Staff had prepared plans and fortifications to defend the Carpathian Mountains, using them as a natural defence line. The Hungarians hoped that they could stop the advancing Red Army at the natural and fortified borderline.

Face with the rapid advance of the Russian forces, the 1st Hungarian Army was mobilised and deployed in the Carpathian Mountains in the spring of 1944. However, the Germans ordered the Hungarians to move the 1st Army out of the well-constructed defence lines of the Carpathian Mountains and into Galicia. The task of the Hungarian forces was to advance and stabilise the situation between the German Army Groups North-Ukraine and South-Ukraine along the line of Kolomea-Ottyina-Stanislavov.

The 1st Army comprised of 3 light infantry (2 regiments each), 3 infantry divisions (with 3 infantry regiments each), two mountain brigades and the 2nd Armoured Division.

The 2nd Armoured Division was mobilised on 13 March and was the most powerful unit of the 1stArmy. The division's artillery was reinforced with the 1st Motorised Medium Howitzer Battalion (31M 150mm howitzers). The division was equipped totally with Hungarian produced armour: 40M, 41M Turán (medium and heavy), 40M Nimród, 39M Csaba and 38M Toldi armoured vehicles. However, due to the slow rate of production, the armoured strength of the division was not at 100%.

The division had 120 medium and 55 heavy Turáns, 84 light Toldi tanks and 42 Nimród A/A vehicles, as well as 14 Csaba armoured cars. Out of the 84 Toldis, 47 were armed with 40mm guns. The 3rd Tank Regiment was short of 18 medium and 14 heavy Turáns, one Toldi and two Nimród armoured vehicles. When the division was deployed to the front, the 3rd Tank Regiment consisted of only two battalions, 3/I and 3/II. The third, (3/III Battalion) remained at home waiting for its armoured vehicles. The 3/III Battalion joined the division at the front line later on.

The artillery and armoured units were transported by rail from 1 April 1944. The majority of the supply column and the 1st Motorised Artillery Battalion arrived to the front only during the operation in April, while the 3/III Tank Battalion only arrived in May, as there were not enough armoured vehicles for them.

The division, commanded by staff Colonel Ferenc Osztovics, reached the assembly area at Stryj, from 5 to 11 of April, 1944. The division then had to move on tracks and wheels 250-300 km from the assembly area to the front line on muddy, snow-covered roads without any rest.

The division began to reassemble into the Lachovce valley on 14 April, and was subordinated to Lieutenant General Lieb, commander of the German XI. Corps.

On that day, the 1st Hungarian Army Command issued its order to XI. German Army Corps, according to which the goal is to reach Nadworna-Stanislau and then Kolomea-Lukwa. The 2nd Armoured Division was intended as the main force of the offensive.

By early dawn of 17 April the Hungarian troops have occupied their starting positions. Two combat groups was formed, named after the commanders (Bercsényi and Sándor), both had one-one tank, motorised rifle, motorised light howitzer battalions and combat support elements.

However that time the 38M Toldi light tanks served at the reconnaissance platoons of the tank companies and battalions, they were not put into the first line to clash with the Soviet T-34 tanks.

Although, the time of the attack was set at 14.00 hours, the units of the 2nd Armoured Division had been in contact with the Soviet forces since 12.00 hours. The units of the Bercsényi Group, while advancing to the starting point, encountered Soviet T-34 tanks in the area of Starunia.

The attacking Hungarian troops captured Nadworna on 18 April and advanced towards Kolomea, but was counter attacked and stopped by the Red Army on 24 April. Both sides went into defence alongside the already captured lines.

From 17 April until 13 May the 2nd Armoured Division suffered the following causalities: 24 tanks were knocked out (9 heavy and 8 medium Turán, 4 Nimród and 2 Csaba), and a further 88 tanks suffered from mechanical failures. Of these, only 6 were non repairable and 7 were captured by the Russians. Altogether 35 armoured vehicles were totally lost and 75 were sent back to repair shops. During the same time, the tanks of the division and the subordinated German armoured units knocked out 48 Russian armoured vehicles. The 3rd Tank Regiment alone destroyed 27 enemy tanks. The personnel casualties of the 2nd Armoured Division totalled 184 killed, 1153 wounded, 112 missing between April 17 and May 13. The 3rd Motorised Rifle Regiment lost 1060 and the 3rd Tank Regiment 384 men.

The Division was withdrawn from the front line and became the reserve of the 1. Army on May 12. General Walter Model, commander of Army Group North-Ukraine, honoured the fighting skills of the Hungarian armoured forces. In May the division was partially re-equipped with German armour to compensate for its losses.

According the official reports of the 2nd Armoured Division, there is no mentioning of the 38M Toldi light tanks as the totally out dated armoured vehicles. Its role was minimised to secure the line of communications, escorting supply convoys and guarding command posts.

In July 1944, the Red Army launched an offensive against the Hungarian lines. The 2nd Armoured Division was put on alert and deployed at Stanislau on 23 July. The Russian forces broke through at Ottyna, where the 3/I Tank Battalion could not stop them.

The 2nd Armoured Division was withdrawn and regroup, after the delayed action of 24-29 July, around Huszt. According to the report of the Division's combat strenght, dated 9 August, it had 14 x 38M Toldi light tanks, 40 x 40M Turán medium

40M Turán medium and 38M Toldi light tanks belonged to the 1st Cavalry Tank Battalion, interestingly the Toldi had a late style military insignia on the frontal plate. [Bonhardt Attila]

Embarkation of the Heavy Company of the 1st Cavalry Tank Battalion at the railway station of Zenta, the air defence of the train was provided by a 38M Toldi light tank with its machine gun on anti aircraft mount. [Pálinkás Zsolt]

38M Toldi IIA light tank belonged to the 1st Cavalry Tank Battalion performing convoy escort duty on the Eastern Front in summer of 1944. [Deák Tamás]

tanks, 14 x 41M Turán heavy tanks, 1-1 Pz. III.M light tank and StuG III G assault gun, 9 x Pz.IV.H medium tanks and three unserviceable Pz.VI.E Tiger heavy tanks. The Tigers were handed back to the Germans

The 1st Cavalry Division in Russia

The 1st Cavalry Division was the pride of the Hungarian Army and the favourite of Regent Horthy. The division was reorganised and reinforced by armour and mechanised artillery units, and after the German occupation of Hungary, this unit was also slated for deployment on the front. The division was mobilised on 29 April 1944.

The Hungarian General Staff wanted to deploy it as a subordinate unit of the 1st Hungarian Army, however the Germans had another plan and the hussars were sent far from other Hungarian units, to the Pripet Marshes. There they initially constituted the reserve of Lieutenant-General Walter Weiss' forces, the German 2nd Army, but within a short time they were thrown into the fray.

The division included the 1st Cavalry Tank Battalion with one heavy and three medium companies plus the staff company, altogether 25 x 38M Toldis, 54 medium 40M Turáns and 11 heavy 41M Turán tanks. Other sources put the totals at 56 medium, 11 heavy Turáns and 5 light Toldi tanks, plus three 38(t) tanks for training. The hussars also had the 3rd Reconnaissance Battalion with two armoured car companies, each with 13 x 39. M Csaba armoured cars. The 15th kBicycle Battalion also had a company of four 40M Nimród Sp. AT/AA vehicles.

Lieutenant Colonel Vilmos Báthory was the commander of the 1st Cavalry Tank Battalion in 1944. The Heavy Company was commanded by Captain Attila Reök.

During the operation the 1st Cavalry Tank Battalion lost all 84 tanks, among them the 38M Toldi light tanks too. According to photographs taken during the operation the Toldi light tanks with 40mm or 20mm armament were used for convoy escorting duties.

The 2nd Armoured Division in Transylvania 1944

Following Romania's change of allegiance in August 1944, the Hungarian General Staff prepared a plan for the occupation of southern Transylvania. The intention was to form a defence line in the southern Carpathian Mountains and so prevent the

Reviewing the troops of the 2nd Armoured Division at Kecskemét in 1943, on the left is a 38M Toldi light tank; one of the command vehicles of 52nd Sp. AA Battalion, on the right is a Mercedes G5 staff car. [Mujzer Péter]

Before the arrival of the medium and heavy Turán tanks, the 3rd Tank Regiment was equipped with 38M Toldi light tanks drive on the streets of Kecskemét in 1942. [Szollár János]

The training of the troops was carried out with 38M Toldi I light tanks at the Armoured Camp of Esztergomtábor to provide manpower for the newly organised tank battalions. [Mujzer Péter]

The obstacle course at Esztergomtábor tried to simulate the diversity of the field conditions to prepare the crew for the combat situation, 38M Toldi I light overcoming the sandy slope. [Mujzer Péter]

38M Toldi I light tank with the late style military insignia rests in the shadow during a summer exercise. That time the 38M Toldi light tanks were organised into the reconnaissance platoons at company and battalion level. [Virág Ajtony]

38M Toldi light tank belonged to the 3/II Tank Battalion crossing the River Bystrica on a makeshift bridge at 17 April 1944 advancing towards Nadworna. The Hungarian sappers still worn the old 17M steel helmets. [ECPA]

Advancing vehicles of the 1st Company of the 52nd Sp. AA Battalion in the bridgehead of Nadworna, in front of the 40M Nimród Sp. AA vehicle is a 38M Toldi light tank/command vehicle; it also has the three digit tactical number 910. [ECPA]

38M Toldi IIA armed with 40mm gun belonged to the 3rd Tank Regiment stuck in the deep mud in Galicia in April 1944, Galicia, in front of the vehicle is a Hungarian field gendarme. [Szollár János]

Russians and their new Romanian allies from advancing into Hungarian territory.

The General Staff quickly organised and mobilised a new 2nd Hungarian Army and reinforced it with the 2nd Armoured Division. The Hungarians launched an offensive against overwhelmingly superior Romanian forces on 5 September.

The Hungarian forces comprised of three reserve infantry divisions, one light infantry division and one infantry division, two reserve mountain brigades, one frontier guard brigade and the 2nd Armoured Division. Facing them in Transylvania was the 1st and 4th Romanian Armies with 20 divisions.

The first stage of attack was successful and the Hungarian forces reached the town of Torda and crossed the Aranyos and Maros Rivers. However, the Russians increased the pace of their advance and successfully blocked the Hungarian drive towards the Carpathians. The Hungarian troops were

38M Toldi I light tank towing a broken down 38M Botond signal truck in Galicia 1944. The Toldi light tank transports a fuel barrel on its engine deck. [Karai Sándor]

Demonstration of the German Pz. V Panther at the Armoured Training Camp of Esztergomtábor. The Hungarians lined up their own tanks too, on the extreme left of the picture is a 38M Toldi light tank. [Szollár János]

forced to withdraw behind the river Maros and prepare for defence.

Taking part in the fighting were the 2nd Armoured Division, the 10th Assault Gun Battalion, and the 101st and 102nd armoured trains. The 2nd Armoured Division led by Major General Zoltán Zsedényi, Colonel László Balsay was the commander of the 3rd Tank Regiment.

Due to the losses suffered in Galicia, the combat strength of the division was depleted. According to the reports it had 14 x 38M Toldi light tanks, 40 x 40M medium Turán, 14 x 41M heavy Turán tanks, 21 x 40M Nimród Sp. AT-AA vehicles and 12 x 39 and 40M Csaba armoured cars. The Division was augmented with one Pz.III, nine Pz.IVH, three Pz.VIH TigerE and one StuG. G armoured vehicles. Around of 4 of September 20 Pz.IVH and five Pz.V Panther tanks arrived to the units.

The 38M Toldi light tanks served at the 3rd Tank Regiment at the reconnaissance platoons and as command vehicles at the Sp.AT-AA companies of 52nd Sp. AT-AA Battalion.

The attack started on 5 September, the Tabay Combat Group, consisted of the 27/III Field Replacement Infantry Battalion, a motorised rifle detachment, one motorcycle platoon, five 38M Toldi light tanks, two 40M Nimród Sp. AA vehicles, the 102nd Armoured Train and four 75mm truck borne mountain guns. The Tabay Group task was to advance in the valley of Maros. The withdrawing Romanian troops blown up the bridge at Marosugar. The advancing Toldis could not cross the river, had to wait the engineers to rebuilt it.

The Toldi light tanks belonged to the Tabay Group reached Dicsőszentmárton on 7 September 1944.

The heaviest fighting took place on 22 September when the Russian-Romanian forces wanted to envelop and destroy the Hungarian defences at Torda.

The attack at 10.30 hours reached the bottom of the valley of Szent János Creek. On the terrain of the Szalonnás Hill - Sósfar Hill one Nimród Company from the 52nd Battalion occupied a blocking position in order to prevent the invading enemy from entering the Sós Valley. Here the Soviet 180th Rifle Division attacked reinforced by the armoured vehicles of the 46th Guard Tank Brigade.

2nd Lieutenant Olivér Várkonyi, company commander of the 52nd Sp. AT-AA Battalion, was in position with five 40M Nimród Sp.AT-AA vehicles and one 38M Toldi command tank. According to Lieutenant Várkonyi, the attack was supported by Su-76 assault guns. When the situation turned to critical, Várkony requested a permit to withdraw. Lieutenant Colonel Jenő Máthé's (commander of the 52nd Sp.AT-AA Battalion) response was short and soldierly: "Hold on, and keep firing!" Várkonyi fought as long as he run out of his ammunition and then withdrew his remaining forces by his own decision. One of his Nimród was knocked out still in the firing position, while the others were shot out during the retreat. They tried to get back to their own troops on foot, but were encircled. Fortunately, the Russian infantry did not notice the small group hiding in the corn field so they came back to their own lines by the night.

38M Toldi I light tank of the 2nd Armoured Division in Transylvania in September 1944. The tank commander stands in front of the tank with the intercom sets in his hand, looks fatigue. [Fortepan]

Operation around Arad in September 1944

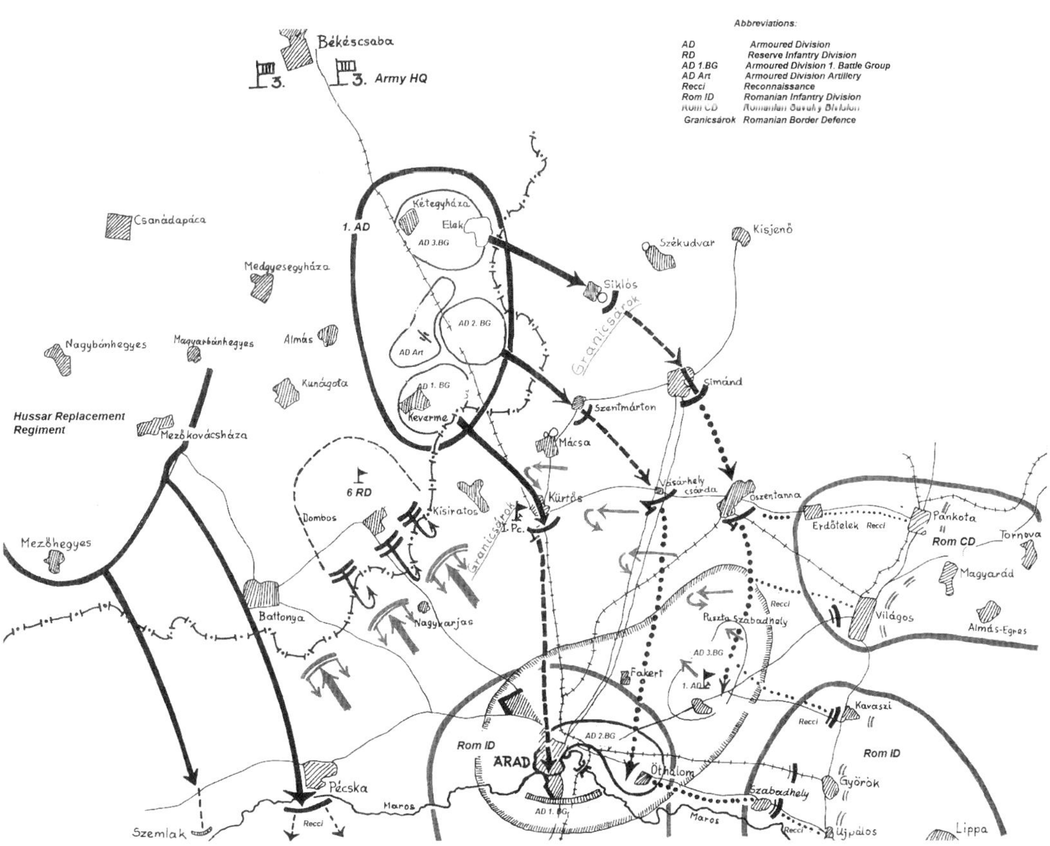

38M Toldi light tanks of the 1/II Tank Battalion led by a Mercedes G5 command car entering into the barracks of Jászberény in 1942.The photos was taken during oath ceremony of the fresh recruits. [Babucs Zoltán]

Reserve officer candidate János Hunyad stands in front of a 38M Toldi light tank of the 1/I Tank Battalion in 1942 at Jászberény, he wears his two pieces 35M leather protective suit and 39M crash helmet with earphone and on his belt the holster for his 37M service pistol. [Babucs Zoltán]

Officers of the 1/II Tank Battalion standing in front of a 38M Toldi light tank, from left to right 2nd Lieutenant Béla Taufer, Captain Ervin Szűcs, 1st Lieutenant Pál Jászi and his wife in May of 1942, Jászberény. [Babucs Zoltán]

38M Toldi I light tank, number plate H-361, painted in dark olive green camouflage and late style white cross military insignia in black square and Mechanised Branch Sign at the Automobile Depot at Mátyásföld 1943. [Fortepan]

According to the Romanian sources, the Romanian forces captured several serviceable Toldi and Turán tanks, two Hetzers and one Zrínyi assault howitzer in Transylvania in September/October 1944. These armoured vehicles contrary to the general rules were used by the Romanian forces against their former owners.

The 2nd Armoured Division in 1944/45

In November 1944 the 2nd Armoured Division was replenished with men and equipment at Komárom. The 3rd Tank Regiment had nine Pz.IV and two 38M Toldi tanks those were serviceable. In second half of November 1944, the 2nd Armoured Division was partially filled up at Párkány. Even at Szákszende, they held conversion training from Turán to Pz.IV tanks.

The 2nd Armoured Division fought at Lovasberény, from 9 to 19 of December.

In early days of December 1944, the Division had 119 armoured vehicles, but only 17 operational. The Division had 26 x 40M Nimród Sp.AT-AA vehicles, 8 x 39M Csaba armoured car, 35 medium 40M Turán tanks, 8 heavy 41M Turán tanks, 16 x 38M Toldi light tanks, one Pz.III, 20 x Pz.IV, four Pz.V Panther tanks and one StuG. III assault gun. By the end of this month 100 armoured vehicles, mostly Hungarian origin was written off.

The 3rd Tank Regiment had three 38M Toldi light tanks, two Pz.IV, and the 52nd AT-AA Battalion had 7 x 40M Nimród armoured vehicles. The Division, with 15 Pz. IV, three motorised rifle battalions and 3 batteries, took part in Operation Conrad I at Székesfehérvár from 7 to 12 January 1945.

By the end of March 1945 the 2nd Armoured Division ceased to exist as a combat unit.

38M Toldi IIA light tank armed with 40mm gun advancing in Transylvania during the operation in September 1944. [Karai Sándor]

Withdrawing bicycle troops and a 38M Botond truck passing a 38M Toldi IIA light tank covering the road at Transylvania autumn of 1944. [Karai Sándor]

1st Armoured Division in 1944/45

The Hungarian IV Corps was organised under Lieutenant General József Heszlényi to block the advance of Russian-Romanian troops on the southern plains of Hungary at Arad and Lippa. The 1st Armoured Division belonged to this force.

The 1st Armoured Division was only partially equipped at this time. The Division was removed from the Order of Battle, when its armament and equipment was handed over to the 2nd Armoured Division, when it was mobilised in April 1944. However the 1st Armoured Division was mobilised again in August of 1944.

The Division consisted of the 1st Tank Regiment with the 1/III Battalion and 1st Motorised Rifle Regiment and one each of reconnaissance, AT/AA, signal, and engineer battalions. The fire support based on an artillery regiment with one rocket-launcher and two artillery battalions. The reconnaissance battalion had one-one armour, motorcycle and motorised rifle company. Due to the depleted organisation and strength the 1st Armoured Division was also called in the official documents as the 1st Armoured Replacement Division.

A Soviet collection point of the enemy vehicles, knocked out 38M Toldi light tank at Budapest at the end of the siege, surrounded by a German Sd.Kfz. half-tracked vehicle and a 41M Turán heavy tank in spring of 1945. [Budapest Ostroma]

An interesting photo of an abandoned 38M Toldi I light tank without turret on the street of Budapest during the siege, it is not clear whether it was the test vehicles of the Toldi tank hunter or the turret was just removed for maintenance. [Budapest Ostroma]

In the autumn of 1944 the 1st Tank Regiment lacked its tanks, so it was necessary to augment them from various training units.

The Division had only one tank battalion commanded by Lieutenant Colonel György Gyurkovich , the 1/III with a staff company (5 x 38M Toldi tanks) and three medium companies (7 x 41M Turán, 5 x 38M Toldi and 3 x 40M Nimród Sp. AT/AA vehicles/ company) as of 2 September 1944.

The 1st Motorised Rifle Regiment commanded by Colonel György Vastagh, had 9 x 40M Nimród and the 51st Sp. AT/AA Battalion had 18 x 40M Nimróds and three 38M Toldi tanks. The 1st Reconnaissance Battalion was commanded by Lieutenant Colonel Imre Németh. The Battalion was lack of the armoured car company and the battalion fire and combat support platoons. It had a mixed armoured car, light tank company where the 39M Csaba armoured cars and 38M Toldi light tanks of the Division were assembled.

The Division had 60-70 armoured vehicles before the start of the operation.

Staff Colonel Ferenc Koszorús led the 1st Armoured Division and Colonel Zoltán Balló commanded the 1st Tank Regiment.

The Hungarian troops planned to attack on September 3, but delayed the offensive until 13 September. Due to this delay the Romanians were able to reinforce their troops and two Romanian infantry divisions and one cavalry division faced the Hungarians, instead of one.

The main goal was to capture Arad, and advance along the Maros Valley up to the Zsil Valley to establish contact with the Hungarian 2nd Army.

The Romanians planned to counter-attack with strong infantry and cavalry formations, but the their troop movements and intention was discovered by a Hungarian reconnaissance aircraft shortly before noon

The 3rd Army commander requested the 1st Armoured Division to begin its offensive, to support the infantry and annihilate the Romanian troops.

The Armoured Division surprised troops of the Romanian 1st Cavalry Division. The Hungarian Turáns attacked and destroyed a large Romanian cavalry group on the road at Macsa-Kürtös. The light tank platoon of 1/8 Mixed Tank Company, commanded by Captain Elemér Gombos, was tasked to occupy the airfield Gáj at the outskirt of Arad. Ensign János Váradi led the 38M Toldi light platoon towards the airfield. The airstrip was surrounded by tall cornfield, and the light platoon stalked the enemy. The Toldi platoon charged the Romanian anti-aircraft artillery positions, wildly firing with their 20mm anti-tank rifles and machine guns. After 20 minutes fire fight the airfield and the 88mm anti-aircraft guns were captured and the German gun crew was liberated.

During 14-17 September 1944, the 1st Armoured Division fought against the 19th Romanian Infantry Division. Due to the terrain the Hungarian forces were forced to attack from head-on. The Hungarian tanks and infantry overran part of the Roman defence line on 16 September. But the following day Soviet armoured columns arrived and helped the Romanian forces to seal the gap. According to Romanian sources, 387 Hungarians were captured and 23 Toldi and Turán tanks knocked out compared to 377 Romanian casualties.

2nd Lieutenant Ferenc Farkas was the son of Colonel General Ferenc Farkas, commissioned as an officer in 1944. He was

Captured 38M Toldi IIA tank prepared for recovery by the Soviet troops in summer of 1944. The recovery vehicle also a captured Hungarian 37M Hansa Lloyd half-tracked artillery tractor. The Hungarian vehicles painted in three tone camouflage. [Sárhidai Gyula]

deployed with the 1st Reconnaissance Battalion, which time it, has a mixed armour company equipped with 38M Toldi light tanks and 39M Csaba armoured cars.

He fought around Orosháza supporting the motorcycle company of the battalion in a fighting withdrawal on 6 October. He lost three Toldi light tank, one was knocked out by the Soviet anti-tank gun, one bogged in a swampy terrain and another had technical brake down. His Toldi tank was hit, but he and his crew could leave the broken vehicle. He was killed in close combat, four days after his arrival to the front, on 8 October 1944 at Szentes. Posthumously he was decorated with the Hungarian Knight Cross with swords.

Siege of Budapest

When the city was encircled, around 24 December a significant Hungarian Army contingent was inside the cauldron. The Hungarian units were either part of the withdrawing 3rd Hungarian Army or originally stationed at Budapest as military units or institutes, schools, depots. The combat strength of the Hungarian troops was added by the various gendarme, police units, voluntary and party security units, plus wandering or lost soldiers without their original units. The divisions were depleted in combat strength, but their artillery was more or less intact.

Approximately, the full strength of the Hungarian forces was about 55000 men. However the members of replacement security battalions, Police forces and military educational institutes never took part in the fighting. The Army only had 38000 troops, but the combatants were about just 15000 men, supported by 250 artillery pieces, 55 heavy anti-tank guns and 37-39 armoured vehicles.

At this time the 1st Armoured Division numbered 5000 men with three field guns, seven tanks and three anti-tank guns and two battalions of infantry.

Between October and early December 1944, the seven assault artillery battalions, in the immediate vicinity of Budapest were grouped under the command of the Billnitzer Group. Only the 1st, 7th, and 10th Assault Artillery Battalions were equipped with assault artillery vehicles. The rest of the assault artillery battalions were armed with a few Turán and Toldi tanks, anti-tank guns and infantry weapons.

The Galánta Gendarmerie Battalion, totalling 500 men led by Major István Szili, was also encircled in Budapest. Its light tank company had ten 35M FIAT Ansaldo and ten 38M Toldi tanks, and ten 39. M Csaba armoured cars.

The Final Battles

Elements of Battle Group Horváth, led by Lt. Col Horváth, fought at Perbál with two Turáns, one Toldi and four Nimróds. Armed with 11 tanks and the remnants of the 7th Assault Gun Battalion, the Group launched a counter-attack at Baracska-Petend on 7 December. The 2nd Cavalry Regiment supported the tanks.

Captured 38M Toldi IIA tank belonged to the 3rd Tank Regiment, the number plate is H-397. This tank is currently exhibited in the Tank Museum of Kubinka. [Sárhidai Gyula]

In 3-4 of December an ad hoc unit was organised on the basis of the mobile warfare class of the Jutasi NCO School. The unit was commanded by 1st Lieutenant György Káplán and had 30 men and two-two 38M Toldi light tank, 40M Nimród Sp.AA_AT vehicles and on 39M Csaba armoured car, training version with iron plated body instead of armoured plates, plus two trucks. The task of the unit was to cover the Margit line and delay the advancing units of the Soviet 5th Guard Cavalry and 16th Tank Corps.

7 December 1944 the unit explored the situation towards Siófok. The leading 38M Toldi was commanded by the unit commander. The totally vulnerable armoured car was at the tail of the column. At the fuel station of Polgárd, the unit was ambushed by Soviet infantry armed with anti-tank rifles. The leading 38M Toldi light tank was immobilised by the anti-tank fire, the drivers injured. 1st Lieutenant Káplán ordered the Nimród Sp. AA-AT vehicles to perform covering fire. The crew was able to leave the Toldi light tank. 1st Káplán ordered the Nimróds to shot into pieces the immobilised Toldi not fallen into enemy hands.

After the war

One of the 38M Toldi reached as far as Bavaria at the end of the war. This Toldi was armed with the experimental 44M rocket launcher, the photo taken by a US sergeant in April-May 1945.

CHAPTER 8

38M Toldi light tank in Soviet service

The Soviet 18th Army established an independent tank battalion based on captured Hungarian materials on 09 September 1944. The 18th Army was able to capture a significant number of enemy tanks. The war booty was repaired on army level and re-enlisted under the red star.

Lt. Gen. Shuravljev, commander of the 18th Army ordered the technical chief of the Army to organise an independent tank battalion with 32 armoured vehicles.

The independent tank battalion numbered 40 officers, 138 NCOs and 28 enlisted men. The battalion consisted of three tank companies, plus the battalion staff and maintenance, support and the medical platoons. The tank companies consisted of three platoons. The battalion had one staff car, two motorbikes, 15 trucks, two tanker trucks and 32 tanks.

At the end of October 1944 the battalion possessed 8 Turáns, 2 Toldi tanks, 3 Zrínyi assault howitzers and 2 Nimród Sp AA/AT vehicles.

Frontal view of the captured 38M Toldi IIA tank belonged to the 3rd Tank Regiment; the number plate is H-397. [Sárhidai Gyula]

The Red Army did not only re-enlist and utilise the captured enemy equipment, it also evaluated it. Guard Col. Voronyinyim, the chief of the maintenance service of the 18th Army summarized his opinion on the captured Hungarian armoured vehicles on 11th November 1944.

The Toldi I, II tanks had smaller engines than the Turán tanks. The Toldi tanks were equipped with one 20 or 40 mm gun and one machine gun. The Toldis were fast, manoeuvrable and easy to drive.

The armoured vehicles listed above were best suited as infantry support. However, these tanks were inferior to the Soviet tanks. Due to their size, they were suitable to overcome narrow, difficult roads.

The evaluated armoured vehicles had very weak armoured protection. Every Soviet AT system could knock them out. The 37mm AT projectiles caused relatively light and easily repairable damage. Projectiles above 37 mm did significant or deadly harm on the Hungarian tanks. The rocket propelled or cumulative shells could easily burn out these vehicles.

After the war just two known copies of the Toldi light tank, one with 20mm and with 40mm guns existing at Kubinka Tank Museum. The 38M Toldi II was captured during the operation at Galicia in summer of 1944, originally belonged to the regimental staff reconnaissance platoon of the 3rd Tank Regiment.

CHAPTER 9

Camouflage and markings of the light tanks in Hungarian service

Camouflage

Initially, the armoured and motor vehicles had no standard camouflage; up to the end of the 1930s each type had a different colour. Later the military vehicles were painted with three-tone standard camouflage.

The Hungarian armoured vehicles manufactured from 1940 were finished in French-style camouflage consisting of a base colour of dark olive green with light ochre and red-brown blotches.

Until 1942, this disruptive camouflage was brush-applied with hard-edged patterns of irregular blotches. However, in 1942 the Hungarians began to use spray equipment on the 38M Toldis and other types, giving the camouflage patterns a more diaphanous appearance. In 1944, some of the armoured and non-armoured vehicles were uniformly painted dark green.

An army regulation defined the camouflage colours to be used, but the style of the patches varied according to the different factories where the vehicles were produced.

National Military Insignia

The first proper, yet unofficial national insignia appeared on the armoured train no.102 during the 1938 campaign in Upper-Hungary/Slovakia. The commander of the train got on his own initiative, the triangular red white-green air force insignia painted on both sides of the gun-wagon, with the tip facing up. After reaching the occupied destination the "selfish" insignia has to be over-painted upon order form high command. Change of policy was brought about in 1940 when Section 31b. of the Ministry of Defence on 16 July ordered armoured units to prepare proposals and designs for a unitary armour insignia. Every unit - the two reconnaissance and the two armoured cavalry battalions - designed and applied to the vehicles their own insignia.

The 1st Reconnaissance Battalion used a white Maltese cross as a base. The green or red outlines and the circle were to be painted in different combinations for each company of the battalion (tankette, light-tank, armoured car). The insignia were painted on all four sides and, for aerial identification, onto the engine deck too. The 38M Toldi tanks and the 39M Csaba armoured cars had the insignia painted onto the turret sides while on the 35M FIAT Ansaldos it was placed on the hull sides. The insignia was painted on all battalion vehicles and was sported during the Transylvanian, Yugoslavian and Ukrainian campaigns. Nevertheless the design was rejected for the sake of "the national insignia must have a univocal and definite meaning" principle.

The vehicles of the 2nd Reconnaissance Battalion had a green cross outlined in white over a red circular base painted on five places. The 38M Toldi tanks of the unit had the fifth insignia on the top of the turret-hatch. This proposal was also rejected, but being similar to the accepted final octagonal insignia, the 2nd Reconnaissance Battalion was allowed to use it up to the end of 1941.

The Mechanised Forces Training- and Instruction-Camp Command suggested the use of a black Maltese cross. The proposal delineated the use of separate unit markings to distinguish the different sub-units. This proposal was also rejected by High Command.

The armoured battalion of the 2nd Cavalry Brigade proposed a white patriarchal cross outlined in red over a green, oval base. This insignia was painted only onto a single 38M Toldi tank.

Finally Mobile Corps Command and the Institute of Military Technology (HTI) jointly developed the octagonal insignia consisting of a green cross outlined in white and the area between the arms of the cross filled with red.

The decision could be delayed no longer because of the imminent start of the Yugoslavian campaign in 1941. Thus following the Chief of Staff's order the last proposal was accepted as follows. The diameter of the insignia should be 500mm, the green lines should be 80mm wide, and the white outline of the cross should be 50mm wide. The insignia should be painted onto the sides, front, rear and the top (engine deck) of vehicles. Whereas the insignia should not fit the intended location, the diameter should be modified to 350mm retaining the original proportions. The insignia in practice resulted to be too large and colourful. The insignia on the hull front, behind which sat the driver on 38M Toldi tanks and 39M Csaba armoured cars, made a perfect aiming-point for enemy anti-tank gunners (enough to think about the heavy white outlines of the cross). Therefore in the field crews often covered the front insignia with mud.

The order issued on 16 November 1942 prohibited the use of the old insignia and introduced a new, uniform one, already used by the air force - white cross over a black square - authorised in three different sizes according to the location on the vehicles. The instructions required the insignia to be placed on all visible sides

The white Maltese cross military insignia developed by the 1st Reconnaissance Battalion in 1940. On the fender the unit sign, a white lightning bolt was painted. [Szollár János]

of vehicles, but in practice it was applied only to the flanks and in increased size to the engine deck. Later of course there were occasions when the required dimensions of the insignia were visibly changed. Some reminiscences recall that on occasions only the white cross was applied without the black square.

While never reached widespread use the national flag fixed over a frame to ease identification both from ground and air deserves mentioning. The size of the flag was 500x500 mm, increased, without the frame, to 1x1 m from 1944 on. Photographical evidences show that it was used on trucks from 1941 too.

Unit Insignia

The first unit signs were painted on the 35M FIAT Ansaldos in 1938; these were white triangles on the training vehicles at Hajmáskér and Táborfalva. During the first mobilisation in 1938, the tankette companies were formed and assigned to the Mixed Brigades. Each unit invented its own colourful unit identification signs. Later, the standard requirements were to use adaptations of easy geometrical symbols, but these instructions did not yet exist when the early units were formed.

The regulations forbade the use of the Hungarian crown, wings or the death's head in a unit insignia. The crown was part of the national insignia, the air force used the wings, and the death's head belonged to the chemical warfare units. Nevertheless, almost all unit insignia incorporated at least one of these symbols.

In 1940, the High Command prohibited the use of any self-made signs on armoured vehicles. Only the 1st and 2nd Reconnaissance Battalions were authorised to use the 1F (plus lightning bolt) and 2F markings on the vehicles.

In 1941 the Mobile Corps units used their own unit signs. However, the deployed 38M Tolid light tanks, 35M FIAT Ansaldos tankettes of the tank and armoured cavalry battalions also worn their original unit signs during the Ukrainian Campaign. According to the original photos we can find 38M Toldi light tanks with white lightning bolt, tank or skulk signs. Some cases the battalion sign was painted on the turret and the original unit sign were left on the hull.

As of 1942 the units started to use the basic geometrical symbols, painted on the front and back mud-guards or the hull.

The Maltese cross was painted on the hull and the turret of the 38M Toldi I light tanks, the cross had different colour outlines symbolising the different companies within the battalion. [Szollár János]

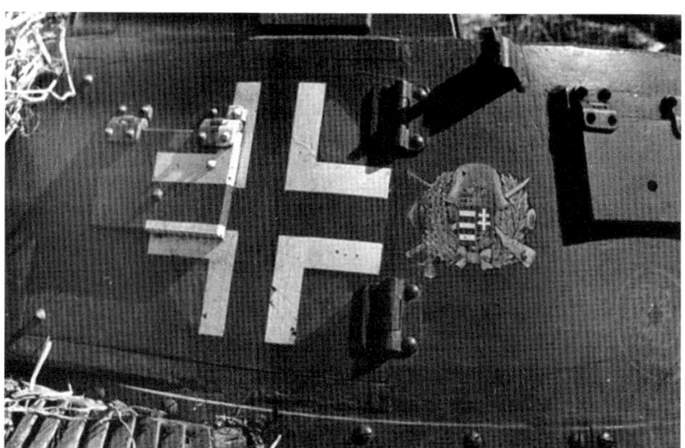

The octagonal military insignia entered service in 1941 and was in effect until the end of 1942. The Mechanised Branch Sign sticker was positioned next to it. [Deák Tamás]

The large scale octagonal military insignia was painted on the frontal armour of the 38M Toldi I light tank, which was a deadly telltale sign for the Soviet anti-tank gunners. On the front lines this insignia was covered with mud to avoid the detection. [Fortepan]

The I Armoured Corps regulated the unit signs of the subordinated units in 1943. Interestingly not all of the units used the regulated unit signs. For example there is no decision in the regulation about the divisional signs for the armoured divisions. The 2nd Armoured Division used the white turned up triangle. According to the original photos, the 2nd Reconnaissance Battalion also used the white German eagle style unit sign instead of the authorised crossed swords in Galicia.

In 1944 the division, regiment and battalion signs were painted on the left and right front and rear hull or mud-guards. The non-armoured vehicles also carried unit signs, following the above mentioned regulations.

The trucks of the armoured battalions carried the same unit signs as the armoured vehicles.

License Plates

The Hungarian Army trucks and armoured vehicles also had a system of vehicle licence plates. The trucks had metal plates, while the armoured vehicles had painted licence plates. On the armoured vehicles, the front serial number was shown in a thin white rectangle. The style was usually an H, with the national shield (red-white-green), followed by a three digit serial number. The capital H referred to the Honvéd (Hungarian Army). The H and the numbers were painted in black. The same serial numbers were on the rear of the hull, but in a square shape.

Later, from 1944, the front license plate was simply painted on the camouflage without the white rectangle. On each license plate, the letters identified the type of vehicle; H for Ansaldos, Toldis, 1H identified the Turán 40M, 2H was the Turán 41M, and 3H was the Zrínyi.

Military trucks carried the same metal licence plates, also with the national shield, capital H and digits. Civilian trucks kept their civilian number plates.

Tactical Numbering

Hungarian armoured vehicles adopted the use of turret numbers in 1942. In 1944 the 2nd Armoured Division used a four-digit tactical number painted only on the rear plate of the turret. According to some sources the 1st Armoured Division also had this four digit tactical system. The armoured units of the 1st Cavalry/Hussar Division had three digit turret numbers.

According to the photo evidence, the 38M Toldi light tanks did not wear the four digit tactical numbers of the 2nd Armoured Division, probably the size of the turret was too small to paint on a visible scale the four numbers. However, the command vehicles of the 52nd Sp. AT-AA Battalion had their 3 digit tactical numbers.

Individual Markings

Individual markings were not typical among the Hungarian armoured troops. It was not regulated but was tolerated by the Army during the war. Even artillery pieces were named after fiancés and girlfriends according to contemporary film footages.

Protective uniforms, personal weapons of the Armoured Troops in WW2

In the early years the secret armoured troops wore one or two-piece mechanic's overalls, several variants were used.

In 1936 armoured troops received their heavy two-piece brown leather 35M uniform. The leather tunic had strapped cuffs and brown crowned buttons and the trousers had strapped ankles. The tunic, by regulation, was worn tucked into the trousers to make movement inside the armoured vehicles easier. However, according to the photos it was mostly worn outside the trousers. The troops had the Italian style 37M leather crash helmet. The helmet was a deep-domed fibre crash helmet covered with black leather. A thick padded rim ran around the crown, and on the rear there was a leather neck-flap which extended backwards from the ears. The Italian helmet was designed without intercom equipment. The Hungarians developed their own version with earphones and brown leather cover and was designated as model 39M.

Under the leather 35M uniform the troops wore their field uniform, which was extremely hot in summer time. In spite of the short falls of the 35M uniform it was used until the end of the war.

38M Toldi light tanks of the Ludovika Military Academy assembled for inspection on a summer exercise, the tactical numbers painted on the fender of the tanks. [Pálinkás Zsolt]

The number plate on the frontal armour was painted into a white rectangle, consisted a big H a shield with national colours and three digit numbers. [Szollár János]

The unit sign of the Light Tank Company of the 1st Armoured Cavalry Battalion, the Turul bird was painted on the commander's cupola hatch too. [Pálinkás Zsolt]

An interesting unit sign combination, the original dead head unit sign which probably belonged to the 3rd Light Tank Company, 9th Bicycle –Light Tank Battalion was over painted by a white tulip of sign of the 11th Tank Battalion at Ukraina in September 1941. [Pálinkás Zsolt]

On the other hand, a new two-piece German armoured uniform style was developed in 1942. It consisted of a smoke-gray short jacket and trousers and was worn with laced-up boots and khaki coloured "Bocskai" field cap or the 37M/39M crash helmets.

Personal weapons

The armoured troopers had their own personal weapons for close protection. Every men of the crew had the 9mm 29M or 37M service pistols manufactured by FÉG Company. Every armoured vehicle was armed with a few 8mm 31M, 35Mcarbines and German 9mm MP-40 and Hungarian 9mm 43M Király submachine pistols, hand grenades for close protection too.

CHAPTER 10

38M Toldi light tank – individual vehicles' history

Abbreviations (explanations)

Cadet School – Csaba Királyfi Mobile Cadet School

Ludovika – Ludovika Military Academy

ROT – Reserve Officer Training Course for Armoured Troops

The combination of the white triangle and tulip was the unit sign of the Armoured Field Battalion organised at Ukraine from the remnants of the tank battalions in September 1941. [War Correspondent Company]

NCO School – Juttasi NCO School (Tiszthelyettes képző)

Armour Camp – Armour Training Camp at Esztergomtábor

Central Depot – Hungarian Army Central Automobile Depot Mátyásföld, Budapest

1st Rec – 1st Reconnaissance Battalion possessing 38M tanks 1940-1941

2nd Rec – 2nd Reconnaissance Battalion possessing 38M tanks 1940-1941

3rd Rec – 3rd Reconnaissance Battalion, belonged to 1st Cavalry Division, probably few 38M for training in 1943

1st Cav – 1st Armoured Cavalry Battalion, possessing 38M tanks in 1940

2nd Cav – 2nd Armoured Cavalry Battalion, possessing 38M tanks in 1940

9th Tank – 9th Bicycle-Light Tank Battalion, deployed in Ukraine, 1941

11th Tank – 11th Bicycle-Light Tank Battalion, deployed in Ukraine, 1941

Armoured Field Battalion – Due to the losses the light tanks of the 9th and 11th Tank battalions were combined into one armoured battalion, 1941, Ukraine

14th, 15th, 16th Cyclist – Cyclist Battalions in transition from cyclist to armoured units possessing a few 38M tanks

1st As. Art. – 1st Assault Artillery Battalion, few 38M tanks used for training

As. Art. Tr. – Assault Artillery Training Unit

31st Tank – 31st Independent Tank Battalion, 1942

32nd Tank – 32nd Independent Tank Battalion, 1942

The tulip unit sign used later on probably painted on 38M Toldi light tanks belonged to training units and schools. [War Correspondent Company]

30th Tank – 30th Tank Regiment belonged to 1st Armoured Field Division, deployed to river Don 1942-1943

30/I Tank – 30/I Tank Battalion belonged to 30th Tank Regiment, 1st Armoured Field Division 1942-1943

30/II Tank – 30/II Tank Battalion belonged to 30th Tank Regiment, 1st Armoured Field Division 1942-1943

51st Sp.- 51st Sp. AA-AT Battalion, 38M tanks used as command vehicles, deployed with 1st Armoured Field Division 1942-1943 and 1st Armoured Division in 1944-1945

52nd Sp. – 52nd Sp. AA-AT Battalion, 38M tanks used as command vehicles, belonged to 2nd Armoured Division

1/I,II,III Tank – 1/I,II,III Tank Battalions belonged to 1st Tank Regiment, 1st Armoured Division 1943-1945

3/I,II,III Tank – 3/I,II,III Tank Battalion belonged to 3rd Tank Regiment, 2nd Armoured Division 1943-1945

3/Tank – 3/ Tank Battalions later renamed to ...

4/ Tank – 4/ Tank Battalions later renamed to ....

3rd Tank – 3rd Tank Regiment deployed to Galicia in 1944

1st Cav Tank – 1st Cavalry Tank Battalion belonged to the 1st Cavalry Division, deployed to the Eastern Front 1944

40mm – 38M Toldi light tank was rearmed with 40mm gun designated 38M Toldi IIB (T-40)

medic – 43M Toldi medical vehicle 1943-1944

bat medic – 38M Toldi battalion's medical vehicle 1942, served with the 30th Tank Regiment at river Don 1942-1943

R-5/a – R-5/a radio with stick antenna

HTI – Military Technical Institute (Haditechnikai Hivatal –HTI)

Ukraine – Took part of the operation in Ukraine with the Mobile Coprs July-October 1941

Voivodina – Took part of the Yugoslavian campaign April 1941 with the Mobile Corps

-1944 Eastern Front – Armoured units deployed with the 1st Cavalry Division to Belorussia- Poland

KO Ukraine – knocked out light tank in Ukraine, 1941

experimental medical vehicles – HTI

* Known photo of the tank

38M Toldi light tank – individual vehicles' history

Number plate	Factory	modifications	1940	1941	1942	1943	1944
H-004 *	Lansdwerk L-60	Swedish prototype					Cadet School
H-005 *	Landswerk L-62	Swedish prototype					medic
H-301 *	MÁVAG		2nd Rec.	9th Tank Ukraine	4/I Tank	4/I Tank	
H-302 *	MÁVAG		2nd Rec.		4/I Tank	3/III Tank	
H-303 *	MÁVAG		2nd Rec.	9th Tank Ukraine	4/I Tank	4/I Tank	
H-304 *	MÁVAG		2nd Rec.		4/I Tank	4/I Tank	
H-305	MÁVAG		2nd Rec.		4/I Tank	4/I Tank	3/III Tank
H-306	MÁVAG		2nd Rec.	2nd Rec., 9th Tank, Ukraine KO	4/I Tank	4/I, 3/III Tank	
H-307	MÁVAG		2nd Rec.	2nd Rec.	4/I Tank	4/I Tank	
Number plate	Factory	modifications	1940	1941	1942	1943	1944
H-308	MÁVAG		2nd Rec.		4/I Tank	1/II,3/III Tank	
Number plate	Factory	modifications	1940	1941	1942	1943	1944
H-309 *	MÁVAG		2nd Rec.	2nd Rec, 9th Tank, Ukraine	4/I Tank	4/I Tank	3/III Tank
H-310 *	MÁVAG		2nd Rec.	2nd Rec.	4/I Tank	4/I Tank	3/III Tank
H-311 *	MÁVAG	40mm gun	2nd Rec.	2nd Rec. 11th Tank	4/I Tank	4/I Tank	1st As. Art
H-312 *	MÁVAG		2nd Rec.		4/I Tank	3/III Tank	1st As. Art
H-313	MÁVAG	modified?	2nd Rec.		4/I Tank	4/I,3/III Tank	3/III Tank, 1st As. Art.
H-314 *	MÁVAG		2nd Rec.	9th Tank, KO Ukraine	4/I Tank	4/I, 3/III Tank	3/III, 1st As. Art
H-315	MÁVAG		2nd Rec.	9th Tank, KO Ukraine	4/I Tank	4/I, 3/III Tank	1st As. Art
H-316 *	MÁVAG		2nd Rec.	2nd,Rec. 9th Tank KO, Ukraine	4/I Tank	4/I Tank	1st As. Art
H-317	MÁVAG	medic	2nd Rec.		4/I Tank	4/I, 3/III Tank	3/III Tank
H-318	MÁVAG		2nd Rec.		4/I Tank	1/I Tank	
H-319	MÁVAG		1st Rec.		1/I Tank	1/I Tank	
H-320 *	MÁVAG		1st Rec.	2nd Rec, 11th Tank, Ukraine, damaged	31st , 1/I Tank	1/I Tank	
H-321 *	MÁVAG	bat. medic	1st Rec.	51st Sp.	1st Cav ,30/I Tank	1/I Tank	
H-322 *	MÁVAG	bat. medic	1st Rec.	51st Sp.	1st Cav , 30/II Tank	3rd Rec.	
H-323 *	MÁVAG		1st Rec.		1/I Tank	1/I Tank	
H-324 *	MÁVAG		1st Rec.	9th Tank	1/I Tank	As. Art. Tr.	
H-325 *	MÁVAG		1st Rec.		1/I Tank	1/I Tank	
H-326 *	MÁVAG		1st Rec.		1/I Tank	As. Art. Tr.	
H-327	MÁVAG	bat. medic	1st Rec.	51st Sp.	2nd Cav., 30/I Tank	3rd Rec.	
Number plate	Factory	modifications	1940	1941	1942	1943	1944
H-328 *	MÁVAG		1st Rec.		1/I Tank	1/I Tank	
H-329	MÁVAG	burned out at Hajmáskér	1st Rec.		1/I Tank	As. Art. Tr.	
H-330 *	MÁVAG		1st Rec.		1/I Tank	As. Art. Tr.	
H-331	MÁVAG		1st Rec.		1/I Tank	1/I Tank	
H-332 *	MÁVAG		1st Rec.	9th Tank Ukraine, damaged	1/I Tank		
H-333 *	MÁVAG		1st Rec.	9th Tank Ukraine	1/I Tank	As. Art. Tr.	
H-334 *	MÁVAG		1st Rec.	Armoured Field Battalion, Ukraine	1/I Tank	As. Art. Tr.	
H-335	MÁVAG	bat. medic	1st Rec.	51st Sp.	30/II Tank		
H-336 *	MÁVAG		1st Rec.	Voivodina	1/I Tank	1/I Tank	
H-337 *	MÁVAG		Ludovika	Ludovika, L 11 turret number			

H-338 *	MÁVAG		2nd Cav.	2nd Cav.		1/II, 3/III Tank	
H-339 *	MÁVAG		2nd Cav.	2nd Cav.		1/II Tank	
H-340	GANZ		2nd Cav.	2nd Cav.	4/I Tank		
H-341	GANZ		1st Cav.		3/I Tank	3/I Tank	
H-342	GANZ		1st Cav.		3/I Tank	3/I Tank	
H-343 *	GANZ		1st Cav.		3/I Tank	3/I Tank	
H-344 *	GANZ		1st Cav.	Voivodina	3/I Tank		
H-345	GANZ		1st Cav.		3/I Tank		
H-346	GANZ		1st Cav.		3/I Tank		
H-347	GANZ	medic	1st Cav.		3/I Tank	3/I Tank	
H-348 *	GANZ		1st Cav.		3/I Tank	3/II Tank, technical failure	repair in Budapest
Number plate	Factory	modifications	1940	1941	1942	1943	1944
H-349	GANZ		1st Cav.		3/I Tank	3/I Tank	
H-350	GANZ		1st Cav.			3/I Tank	
H-351	GANZ	medic	1st Cav		3/I Tank	3/I Tank	
H-352	GANZ		1st Cav		3/I Tank	3/I Tank	
H-353	GANZ		1st Cav			3/I Tank	
H-354	GANZ		1st Cav		burned out	3/I Tank	
H-355 *	GANZ		1st Cav		3/I Tank	1/II Tank	
H-356 *	GANZ	medic	1st Cav	9th Tank, Ukraine		3/I Tank	
H-357 *	GANZ		1st Cav	burned out		3/I-II Tank	
H-358	GANZ	medic	1st Cav		3/I Tank	3/II Tank	
H-359	GANZ		2nd Cav		2/I Tank		
H-360 *	GANZ		2nd Cav	2nd Cav	2/I Tank		
H-361 *	GANZ		2nd Cav	11th Tank, Ukraine	2/I Tank	Central Depot 2/I Tank	
H-362 *	GANZ		2nd Cav		2/I Tank		
H-363 *	GANZ		2nd Cav		2/I Tank		
H-364 *	GANZ		2nd Cav		2/I Tank		
H-365 *	GANZ		2nd Cav		2/I Tank		
H-366 *	GANZ		2nd Cav		2/I Tank	2/I Tank	
H-367	GANZ		2nd Cav		2/I Tank	1/III Tank	
H-368	GANZ		2nd Cav		2/I Tank		
H-369	GANZ		2nd Cav		2/I Tank		
Number plate	Factory	modifications	1940	1941	1942	1943	1944
H-370 *	GANZ		2nd Cav		2/I Tank		
H-371	GANZ		2nd Cav		2/I Tank		
H-372	GANZ		2nd Cav		2/I Tank		
H-373	GANZ		2nd Cav		2/I Tank		
H-374 *	GANZ		2nd Cav	11th Tank	2/I Tank		
H-375 *	GANZ		2nd Cav	11th Tank, Ukraine	2/I Tank		
H-376 *	GANZ		2nd Cav	11th Tank Ukraine, KO	2/I Tank		
H-377 *	GANZ		Central Depot	1st Cav Ukraine	31st Tank	3/I, II Tank	
H-378	GANZ		Central Depot	1st Cav	31st Tank	3rd Rec	
H-379 *	GANZ		Central Depot	1st Cav Ukraine	31st Tank	3rd Rec, ROT	

H-380 *	GANZ		Central Depot	1st Cav Ukraine	31st Tank	3rd Rec	
H-381 *	MÁVAG			Ukraine 16th Cyclist		burned out,written off	
H-382	MÁVAG			2nd Cav	32nd , 3/I Tank		
H-383 *	MÁVAG			2nd Cav	31st Tank		
H-384	MÁVAG	40mm?		2nd Cav	1/II Tank	51st Sp	1st Cavalry Tank 1944 Eastern Front
H-385	MÁVAG			15th Cyclist	31st Tank	1st Cav Tank	
H-386	MÁVAG	40mm gun		14th Cyclist		1st Cav Tank, 1st As. Art.	
H-387	MÁVAG					1st Cav Tank	
H-388	MÁVAG					1st Cav Tank	
H-389	MÁVAG					1/II Tank	
H-390 *	MÁVAG			Ukraine KO	Jászberény	1/II Tank	
Number plate	Factory	modifications	1940	1941	1942	1943	1944
H-391 *	MÁVAG	40mm gun		Ukraine		1/II Tank,1st As Art	
H-392	MÁVAG	40mm gun		Ukraine	31st Tank	1st As. Art.	
H-393	MÁVAG				31st Tank		
H-394	MÁVAG					1/II Tank	
H-395	MÁVAG					1/II Tank	
H-396	MÁVAG				31st Tank	1/II Tank	
H-397 *	MÁVAG			9th Tank, KO Ukraine	31st Tank	1/II Tank	3rd Tank captured in Galicia
H-398	MÁVAG				31st Tank	1/II Tank	
H-399 *	MÁVAG			9th Tank, KO Ukraine		repair	
H-400	MÁVAG	40mm gun				1/I Tank, 1st As. Art.	
H-401	MÁVAG	experimental medic vehicle		HTI	Central Depot		
H-402	MÁVAG	40mm gun?				1/II Tank	
H-403	MÁVAG				3/I Tank		
H-404	MÁVAG				3/I Tank		
H-405	MÁVAG				3/I Tank		
H-406	MÁVAG	40mm gun?					1/I Tank, 51st SP
H-407	MÁVAG				3/I Tank		
H-408	MÁVAG				31st Tank	KK	
H-409	MÁVAG					KK	
H-410	MÁVAG				3/I Tank	3/I Tank	
H-411	MÁVAG			9th , 31st Tank	31st , 1/II Tank	1/II Tank	
Number plate	Factory	modifications	1940	1941	1942	1943	1944
H-412	MÁVAG			9th , 31st Tank	31st Tank	1/II Tank	
H-413	MÁVAG			9th , 31st Tank	31st Tank		
H-414	MÁVAG			9th , 31st Tank	31st Tank		
H-415 *	MÁVAG			9th , 31st Tank	31st 1/II Tank		
H-416	MÁVAG			9th , 31st Tank	31st , 1/II Tank	1/II Tank	
H-417 *	MÁVAG				31st Tank	Central Depot	
H-418	MÁVAG			31st Tank	Central Depot , 30th Tank		
H-4019	MÁVAG			31st Tank	Central Depot , 30th Tank		
H-420	MÁVAG			31st Tank	Central Depot, 30th Tank		
H-421	MÁVAG			31st Tank	Central Depot, 30th Tank		

H-422	MÁVAG			31st Tank	Central Depot, 30th Tank	3rd Rec	
H-423 *	GANZ	upgraded armour plates, skirts		Ukraine, 32nd Tank	32nd , 3/II Tank	HTI	
H-424	GANZ			11th Tank	32nd , 3/II Tank	Armour Camp	
H-425	GANZ				32nd , 3/II Tank		
H-426	GANZ				32nd , 3/II Tank	3/II Tank	
H-427	GANZ				3/II Tank		
H-428 *	GANZ	modification?, L 33 turret number			32nd , 3/II Tank	3/II Tank	
H-429	GANZ	modification?			32nd , 3/II Tank	3/II Tank	
H-430	GANZ				32nd , 3/II Tank		
H-431	GANZ				32nd , 3/II Tank	3/II Tank	
H-432	GANZ				32nd , 3/II Tank		
Number plate	Factory	modifications	1940	1941	1942	1943	1944
H-433	GANZ				32nd , 3/II Tank		
H-434 *	GANZ	40mm gun			32nd , 3/II Tank		
H-435	GANZ				32nd , 3/II Tank	3/II Tank	
H-436	GANZ				32nd , 3/II Tank	3/II Tank	
H-437	GANZ					Ludovika	
H-438	GANZ				Ludovika	Ludovika	
H-439	GANZ	modification?			Ludovika	Ludovika	
H-440 *	GANZ	modification?			32nd Tank, Armoured Camp	Ludovika	
H-441	GANZ	modification?			32nd , 3/II Tank	Armour Camp	
H-442	GANZ				3/II Tank		
H-443	GANZ				3/I Tank	3/I Tank	
H-444	GANZ					1st Cav. Tank	
H-445	GANZ					Central Depot	
H-446	GANZ				4/I Tank	4/I Tank	
H-447 *	GANZ			9th , 31st Tank,	31st 1/II Tank		
H-448	GANZ			9th , 31st Tank		1/II Tank	
H-449	GANZ			11th Tank	32nd , 3/II Tank		
H-450	GANZ			11th Tank	3/II Tank		
H-451	GANZ			11th Tank	32nd , 3/II Tank	Central Depot	
H-452	GANZ	Toldi III experiment		11th Tank	32nd , 3/II Tank		
H-453 *	GANZ			11th Tank	32nd , 3/II Tank		
Number plate	Factory	modifications	1940	1941	1942	1943	1944
H-454	GANZ			11th Tank	32nd , 3/II Tank		
H-455 *	GANZ	modification?	Armoured Camp	11th Tank	32nd , 3/II Tank	1st Cav. Tank	
H-456 *	GANZ			11th Tank	32nd , 3/II Tank	3/ Tank	
H-457	GANZ	R-5/a		31st Tank	Central Depot, 30th Tank	3rd Rec.	
H-458	GANZ	40mm gun		31st Tank	31st Tank, Central Depot	1st. As. Art.	
H-459	GANZ	R-5/a		31st Tank	Central Depot, 30th Tank	3rd Rec.	
H-460	GANZ	R-5/a		31st Tank	Central Depot, 30th Tank		
H-461	GANZ	40mm gun			NCO School	NCO School	
H-462	GANZ	40mm gun			NCO School	NCO School	

H-463	GANZ				Cadet School	Cadet School, Ludovika	
H-464 *	GANZ						
H-465 *	GANZ				Cadet School	Cadet School	
H-466	GANZ					NCO School	
H-467	GANZ	40mm gun				NCO School	
H-468	GANZ	40mm gun				NCO School	
H-469 *	GANZ	40mm gun				NCO School	
H-470	GANZ	40mm gun				NCO School	
H-471	GANZ					Ludovika	
H-472	GANZ				Ludovika	Ludovika	
H-473 *	GANZ	modification?			Ludovika	Ludovika	
H-474	GANZ				Ludovika	Cadet School	
Number plate	Factory	modifications	1940	1941	1942	1943	1944
H-475	GANZ					Ludovika	
H-476	GANZ				Ludovika	Ludovika	
H-477	GANZ					Ludovika	
H-478 *	GANZ					Ludovika, L 33 turret nr.	
H-479	GANZ			51st Sp.			
H-480	GANZ			51st Sp.			
H-481	GANZ			51st Sp.			
H-482	GANZ			51st Sp.			
H-483 *	GANZ	Toldi III, experimental turret				HTI	
H-484	GANZ				4/I Tank		
H-485	GANZ				4/I Tank	3/III Tank	
H-486	GANZ	modification?				Central Depot	
H-487	GANZ					Central Depot	
H-488	GANZ				3/I Tank	3/I Tank	
H-489	GANZ	modification?				Central Depot	
H-490	GANZ	modification?				Central Depot	

Bibliography

A M. kir. Fegyveres erők képeskrónikája (1919-1945), Vitézi Szék, 1977
„Álltak Tordánál a csatát fejtőig vérben", Emlékkönyv a tordai csata 60. évfordulójára, 2004 Torda
Babucs Zoltán: Jászsági honvédek a II. világháborúban, I. A jászberényi harckocsi zászlóalj története a II. világháborúban, 2000
Babucs Zoltán – Maruzs Roland: „Jász vitézek rajta, előre!" A jászberényi kerékpáros és harckocsizó zászlóalj története 1920-1944, Puedlo
Bene János: Nyíregyházi katonaság a II. világháborúban 1938-1945, Jósza András Múzeum 2016
Bíró Ádám – Éder Miklós – Sárhidai Gyula: A magyar királyi honvédség külföldi gyártású páncélos harcjárművei 1920- 1945, Petit Real, 2006
Bíró Ádám – Éder Miklós – Sárhidai Gyula: A magyar királyi honvédség hazai gyártású páncélos harcjárművei 1920- 1945, Petit Real, 2012
Bombay László: A harckocsik története, Akadémia, 1990
Bombay László – Gyarmati József – Turcsányi Károly: Harckocsik 1916-tól napjainkig, Zrínyi
Bonhardt Attila – Sárhidai Gyula – Winkler Róbert: A magyar királyi honvédség fegyverzete 1919-45 part 1, Zrínyi, 1992
Dombrády Loránd-Tóth Lajos: Magyar Királyi Honvédség 1919-45, Zrínyi, 1987
Dombrády Loránd: A magyar gazdaság és a hadfelszerelés, 1938/44, Akadémia, 1981
Csernavölgyi Antal : Az aranycsillag rabjai, Pécs 1994
Csima János: Források a Magyar Honvédség II. világháborús történetének tanulmányozásához, Zrínyi, 1961
Hajdú Ferenc – Sárhidai Gyula: A magyar királyi honvéd Haditechnikai Intézettől a HM Technológiai Hivatalig, HM Technológiai Hivatal 2005
Horváth Csaba – Lengyel Ferenc: A délvidéki hadművelet 1940, Puedlo
Illésfalvi Péter – Szabó Péter – Számvéber Norbert: Erdély a Hadak Útján 1940-1944, Puedlo
Magyarország a II. világháborúban, Enciklopédia, PETIT REAL, 1997
Maruzs Roland: Középkereszt, tisztikereszt, lovagkereszt, Zrínyi, 2013
Páncélos csapatok 60. Évfordulója, HM, 1996
Mujzer Péter: PÁNCÉLOSOK, A magyar páncéloscsapatok és rohamtüzérség története 1938-1945, Magánkiadás 2019
Szabó Péter – Számvéber Norbert: A keleti hadszíntér és Magyarország 1941- 1943, Puedlo
Szabó Péter – Számvéber Norbert: Magyarország és a keleti hadszíntér 1943-1945, Puedlo
Rada Tibor: A magyar királyi honvéd Ludovika Akadémia és testvérintézetek összefoglaló története 1930-1945, GÁLOS NYOMDÁSZ Bt, 1998
Ravasz István: Erdély, mint hadszíntér 1944, PETIT REAL, 1997
Stark Tamás: Hadak Útján, Corvina, 1991
Ungváry Krisztián: A magyar honvédség a második világháborúban, Osiris, 2005
Veress D. Csaba: Magyarország hadikrónikája 1944-1945 I.-II.
Militaria 2002

Articles
ZMKA Akadémiai Közlemények:
Horváth Csaba: A Gyorshadtest felderítő szolgálata a
Jugoszlávia elleni háborúban, 1991/182
Dr. Lengyel Ferencz: M. kir. I. Gyors Hadtest hadműveletei a Szu elleni háborúban 1941 július 9. november 15., 1994/204
Hadtörténeti Közlemények:
Tóth Lajos: A Gyorshadtest a Szovjetunióban, HK 1966/2
Dombrándy Loránd: A horthysta katonai vezetés erőfeszítései a páncélos fegyvernem megteremtésére, HK 1969/2, 1970/4
Haditechnikai Szemle:
Bíró Ádám: Az első magyar tervezésű harckocsi a V-4, 1992/4
Bíró Ádám: Magyar, Marder páncélvadász Toldi alvázon, 1990/4
Dr. Klemensits Péter: A magyar páncélos alakulatok a kárpátaljai hadműveletekben 1., 2014/5
Dr. Klemensits Péter: A magyar páncélos alakulatok a délvidéki hadműveletekben, 2014/6
Dr. Klemensits Péter: A Magyar páncélos erők a Szovjetunió elleni hadműveletekben – a Toldi könnyű harckocsi I. rész, 2016/1
Dr. Klemensits Péter: A Magyar páncélos erők a Szovjetunió elleni hadműveletekben – a Toldi könnyű harckocsi II. rész, 2016/2
Dr. Mujzer Péter: A magyar páncélos fegyvernem kezdetei I. rész, 2016/1
Dr. Mujzer Péter: A magyar páncélos fegyvernem szervezeti és fegyverzeti fejlesztése 1938-1942 I. rész, 2016/2
Dr. Mujzer Péter: A magyar páncélos fegyvernem szervezeti és fegyverzeti fejlesztése 1938-1942 II. rész, 2016/3
Dr. Mujzer Péter: A Magyar Királyi honvédség páncélos csapatainak végső szervetete 1942-1944, 2016/4
Dr. Mujzer Péter: A Magyar Királyi Honvédség páncélos csapatainak képzési rendszere, 2016/5
Dr. Mujzer Péter: Magyar páncélosok alkalmazása a II. világháborúban I. rész, 2016/6
Dr. Mujzer Péter: Magyar páncélosok alkalmazása a II. világháborúban II. rész, 2017/1
Dr. Mujzer Péter:A Magyar Királyi Honvédség páncélos szervezeteinek részvétele a Szovjetunió elleni hadműveletekben 1941-ben, 2017/3
Dr. Mujzer Péter: Magyar páncélos csapatok a keleti fronton 1942-43, I. rész, 2017/4
Dr. Mujzer Péter: Magyar páncélos csapatok a keleti fronton 1942-43 II. rész, 2017/5
Dr. Mujzer Péter: A 2. páncéloshadosztály hadműveletei Galiciában 1944-ben, I. rész, 2017/6
Dr. Mujzer Péter: A 2. páncéloshadosztály hadműveletei Galiciában 1944-ben, II. rész, 2018/1
Dr. Mujzer Péter: A magyar megszálló erők páncélos alakulatai, 2018/2
Dr. Mujzer Péter: Az 1. lovas-, a későbbi huszárhadosztály páncélos alakulatai a keleti fronton, 1944-ben, 2018/3
Somkutas Róbert: A Magyar Királyi Honvédség páncélozott eszközökkel felszerelt felderítő csapatai I. rész, 2016/1
Somkutas Róbert: A Magyar Királyi Honvédség páncélozott eszközökkel felszerelt felderítő csapatai II. rész, 2016/2
Somkutas Róbert: A Magyar Királyi Honvédség páncélozott eszközökkel felszerelt felderítő csapatai III. rész, 2016/3
Somkutas Róbert: A Magyar Királyi Honvédség páncélozott eszközökkel felszerelt felderítő csapatai IV. rész, 2016/4
Somkutas Róbert: A Magyar Királyi Honvédség páncélozott eszközökkel felszerelt felderítő csapatai V. rész, 2016/5
Somkutas Róbert: A Magyar Királyi Honvédség páncélozott eszközökkel felszerelt felderítő csapatai VI. rész, 2016/6
Somkutas Róbert: A Magyar Királyi Honvédség páncélozott eszközökkel felszerelt felderítő csapatai VII. rész, 2017/2
Somkutas Róbert: A Magyar Királyi Honvédség páncélozott eszközökkel felszerelt felderítő csapatai VIII. rész, 2017/3
Somkutas Róbert: A Magyar Királyi Honvédség páncélozott eszközökkel felszerelt felderítő csapatai IX. rész, 2017/4
Somkutas Róbert: A Magyar Királyi Honvédség páncélozott eszközökkel felszerelt felderítő csapatai X. rész, 2017/5
Somkutas Róbert: A Magyar Királyi Honvédség páncélozott eszközökkel felszerelt felderítő csapatai XI. rész, 2017/6
Katona Újság
Simon Tamás: Az 1. gépkocsizó dandár a nyikolajevi csatában, 2013/4.
Belvedere
GALLó Krisztián: Páncélosok a Kárpátokban, 2003/XV. 1-2, 3-4., 5-6.

Militaria Modell:
Éder Miklós: Magyar páncélos járművek alakulat jelzései, 1. rész, 1991 / 1
Éder Miklós: Magyar páncélos járművek alakulat jelzései, 2. rész, 1991/2
Éder Miklós: 38M Toldi könnyűharckocsi, 1991/3
Éder Miklós: Magyar páncélos csapatok bőrruházata, 1992/4
Éder Miklós: Magyar páncélosok hadi jelzése, 1917-1945, 1992/6

Pro Modell

Mujzer Péter: A magyar királyi honvédség páncélos csapatainak jelzésrendszere, 2003/1-3

Foreign Books

David Ansell: Military Motorcycles, Osprey, 1996

Max Axworthy: Third Axis Fourth Ally, Arms and Armour, 1995

Dr Tamás Baczoni – Dr László Tóth: Hungarian Army Uniforms 1939 – 1945, HUNIFORM 2010

Csaba Becze: Magyar steel, Mashroom Publication, 2006

Dénes Bernád, Charles K. Kliment: Magyar Warriors, The history of the Royal Hungarian Armed Forces 1919-1945, volumen 1, Helion Publication, 2015

Dénes Bernád, Charles K. Kliment: Magyar Warriors, The history of the Royal Hungarian Armed Forces 1919-1945, volumen 2, Helion Publication, 2017

Patrick Cloutier: Three Kings: Axis Royal Armies on the Russian Front 1941, 2014

Peter Gosztonyi: Deutschlands waffengefahrten an de rost front 1941-1941, Motorbuch Verlag, 1981

George Forty: World War Two Tanks, Osprey, 1996

Janusz Ledwoch: Eastern Front 1941-45, Militaria, 1995

Victor Madej: South-Eastern Europe Axis Armies Handbook, Game Marketing Company, 1982

Military Intelligence Division: Order of Battle and Handbook of the Hungarian Armed Forces, 1944 US War Dep. (restricted)

Eduardo Gil Martinez: Fuerzas Acorazadas Húngaras 1939-43, Almena 2017

Péter Mujzer: Hungarian Mobile Forces 1920-45, Bayside Books, 2000

Péter Mujzer: Huns on Wheels, Hungarian Mobile Forces in WWII, Armoured, Cavalry, Bicycle Troops, Motorised Rifle, Mujzer and Partners Ltd., 2015

Péter Mujzer: Hungarian Armoured Forces in WWII, KAGERO Books, PHOTOSNIPER 26., 2017

Péter Mujzer: Hungarian Armoured Troops in WWII, KAGERO Books, PHOTOSNIPER 28., 2018

Leo Niehorster: The Royal Hungarian Army 1920-45, Bayside Books, 1998

Yurij Pasholok: L-60: Scandinavian Tank Revolution www.tankarchives.ca/2016/09/l-60-scandinavian-tank-revolution.html

Aleksandr Sirota: Toldi: The Hungarian Light Knight www.tankarchives.ca/2016/10/toldi-hungarian-light-knight.html

Janusz Pielkalkiewicz: The Cavalry 1939-45, Macdonald, 1986

Janusz Pielkalkiewicz: Tank War 1939-1945, Guild Publishing, 1986

Jean Restayn: WWII tank encyclopedia in color 1939-1945, Histoire&Collection

Ronald Tarnstrom: Balkan Battles, Trogen Books, 1998

Nigel Thomas- László Pál Szabó: The Royal Hungarian Army in World War II, Ospery, 2008

Anthony Tucker-Jones: Armored warfare and Hitler's allies 1941-1945, Pen&Sword, 2013

Steven Zaloga- James Grandsen: The Eastern Front, Arms and Armour, 1983

Steven Zaloga: Tanks of Hitler's eastern allies 1941-45, Osprey, 2013

Charles Winchester: Ostfront, Hitlers war on Russia 1941-1945, Osprey, 1998

38M Toldi light tank belonged to the 9th Tank Battalion, Jászberény still wearing the Turul bird unit sign of the Light Tank Company of the 1st Armoured Cavalry Battalion. [Babucs Zoltán]

The original Order of Battle of the armoured units equipped with 38M Toldi light tanks

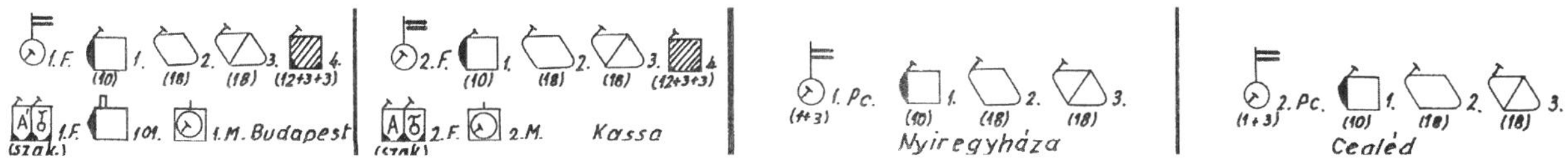

– 1.F – 1st Reconnaissance Battalion 1940; – 2.F – 2nd Reconnaissance Battalion 1940; – 1.Pc – 1st Armoured Cavalry Battalion 1940; – 2.Pc – 2nd Armoured Cavalry Battalion1940 (in each OB of the 1940 the second rhomboid sign means the light tanks and the numbers)

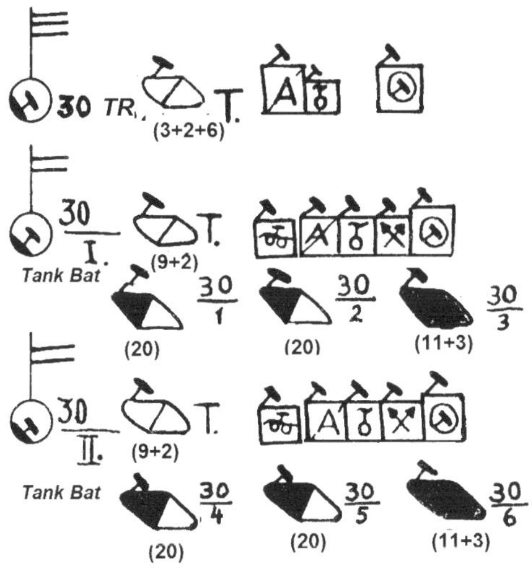

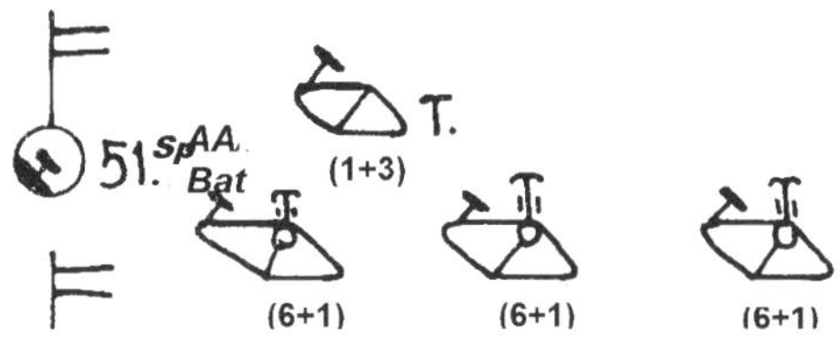

- 30 TR -30th Tank Regiment 1942 (in the bracket the second digit means the 38M Toldi light tanks)
- 30/I and II Tank Bat – 30/I and II Tank Battalions 1942 (in the bracket the second digit means the 38M Toldi light tanks at the battalion staff)
- 51. Sp AA Bat – 51st Sp. AA Battalion 1942 (in the bracket the second digit means the 38M Toldi light tanks at the staff and the companies too)

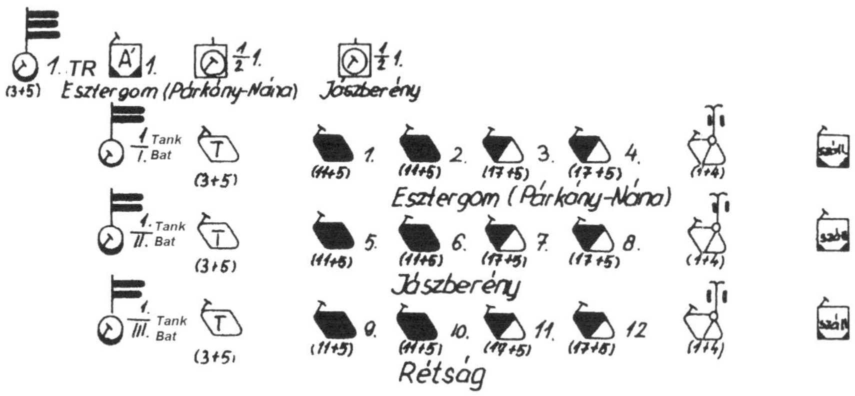

- 1. TR – 1st Tank Regiment
- 1/I, II, III Tank Bat. – 1/I, II, III Tank Battalions (Every level in the bracket the 5 means the number of the 38M Toldi light tanks at the reconnaissance platoons, the Sp. AA platoons also has one 38M Toldi command vehicles)

- 51. AA/AT Bat – 51st Sp. AA-AT Battalion (in the brackets the first digit means the 38M Toldi command vehicles)

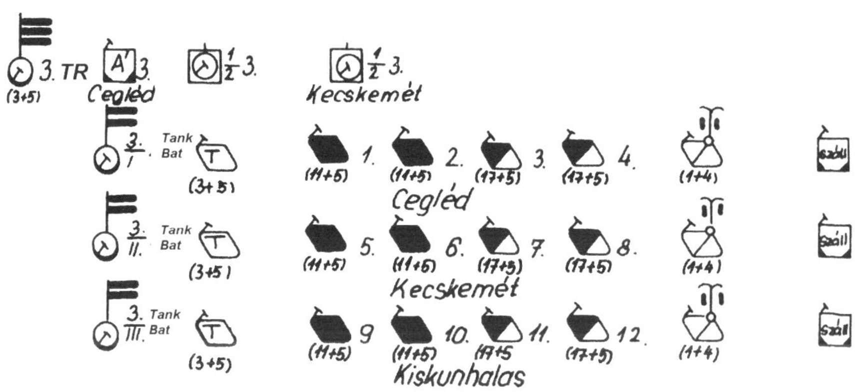

- 3. TR – 3rd Tank Regiment
- 3/I, II, III Tank Bat.- 1/I, II, III Tank Battalions (Every level in the bracket the 5 means the number of the 38M Toldi light tanks at the reconnaissance platoons, the Sp. AA platoons also has one 38M Toldi command vehicles)

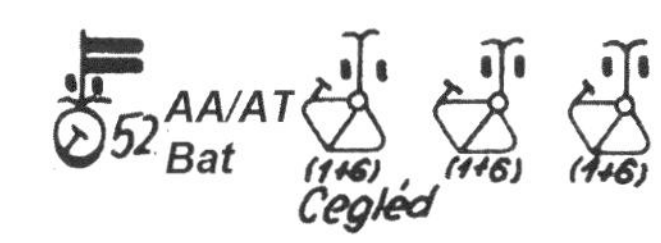

- 52. AA/AT Bat – 52nd Sp. AA-AT Battalion (in the brackets the first digit means the 38M Toldi command vehicles)

- 1. Cavalry Tank Battalion – 1st Cavalry Tank Battalion (at the rhomboid unit sign with T means Staff Company in the brackets the second digit means the 38M Toldi light tanks of the reconnaissance platoon)

Four view of the 38M Toldi I light tank [drawings Bajtos Iván]

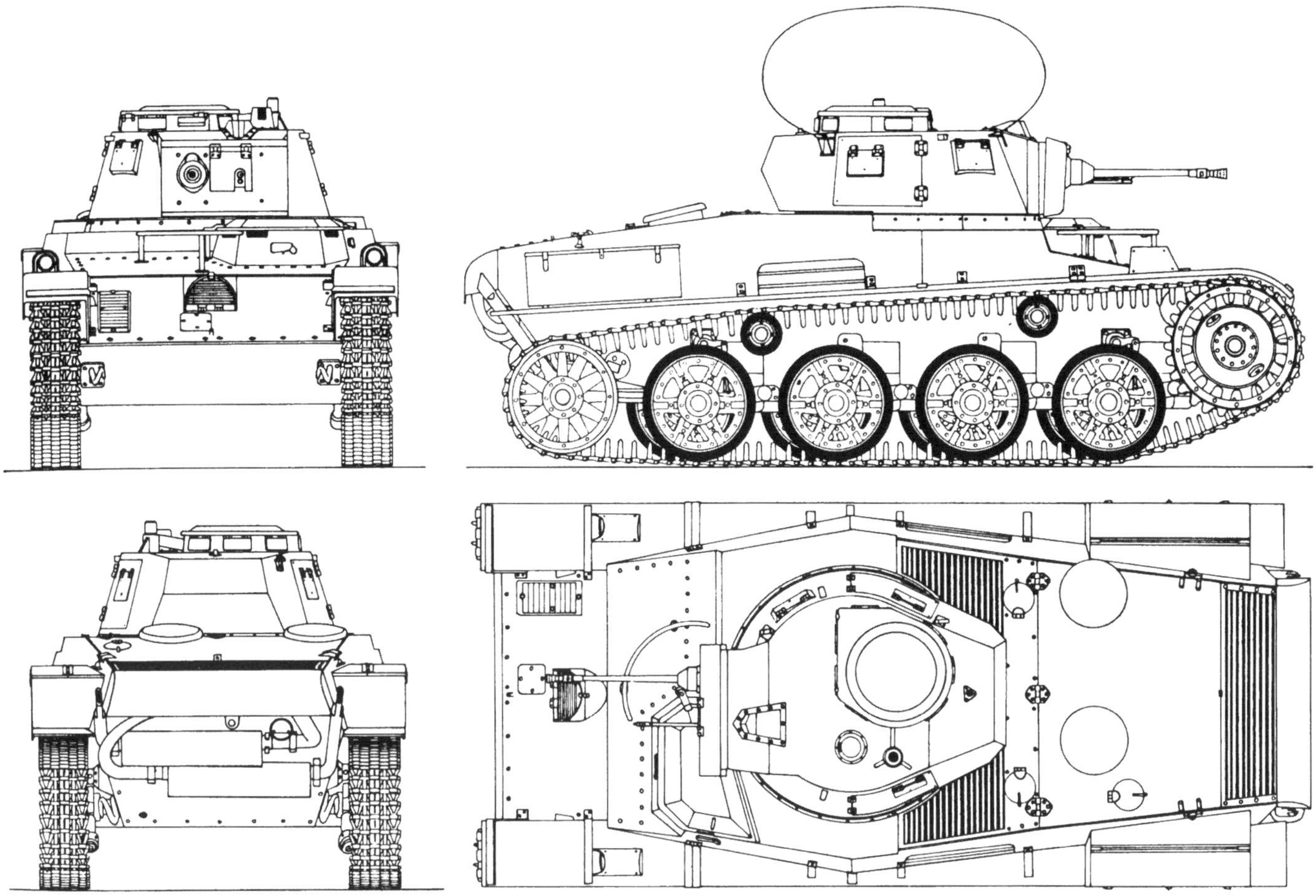

Four view of the 38M Told IIA light tank

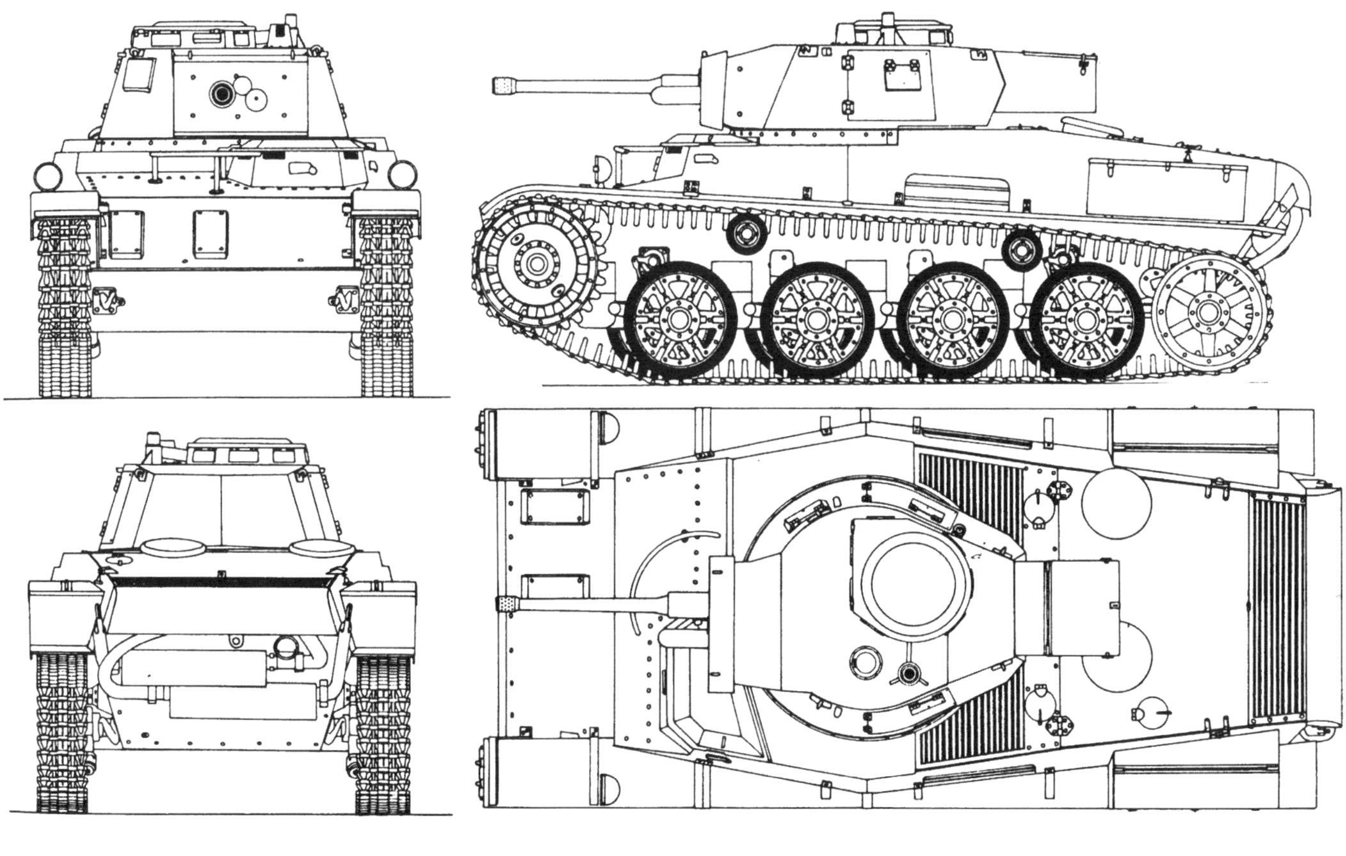

Four view of the 38M Toldi III light tank

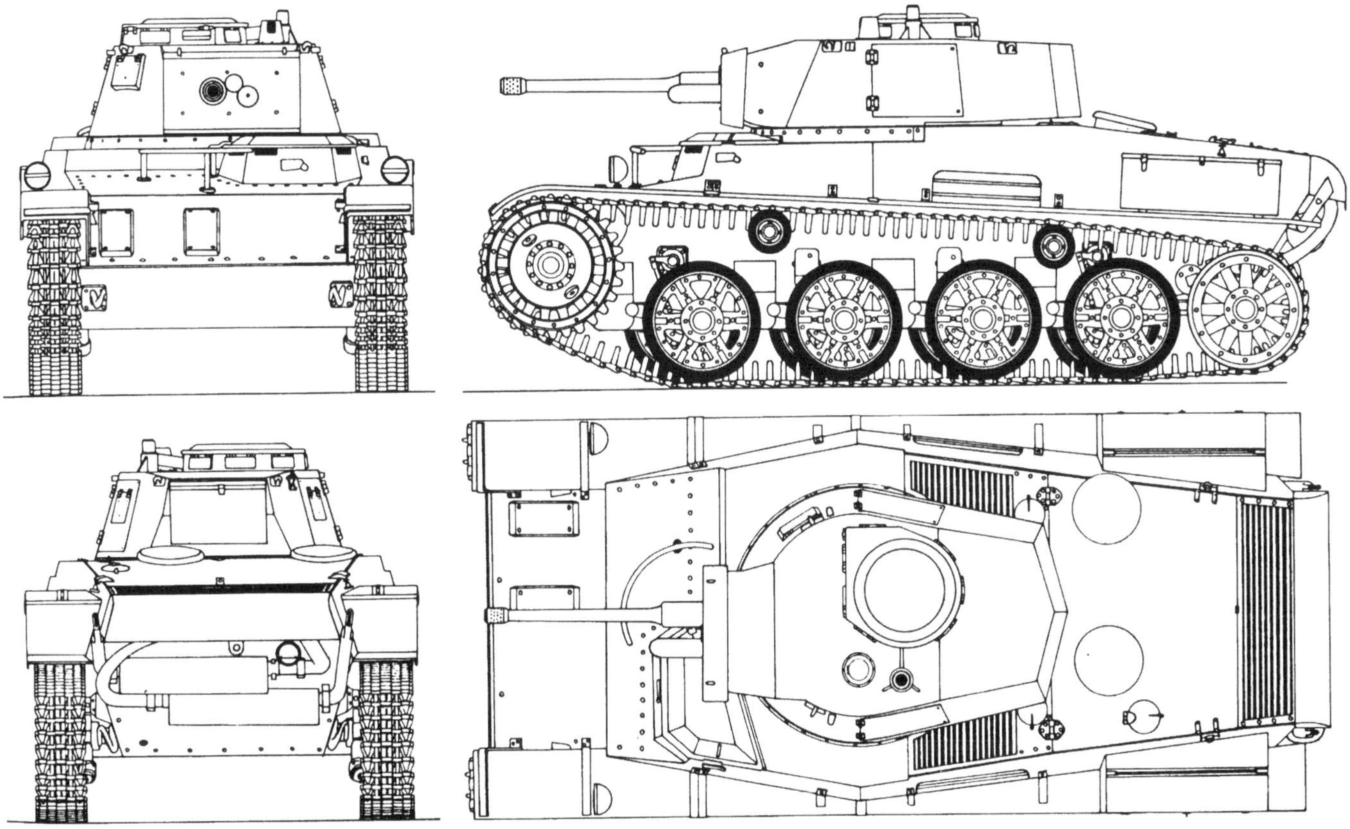

Frontal and side view of the skirt plated 38M Toldi IIA light tank

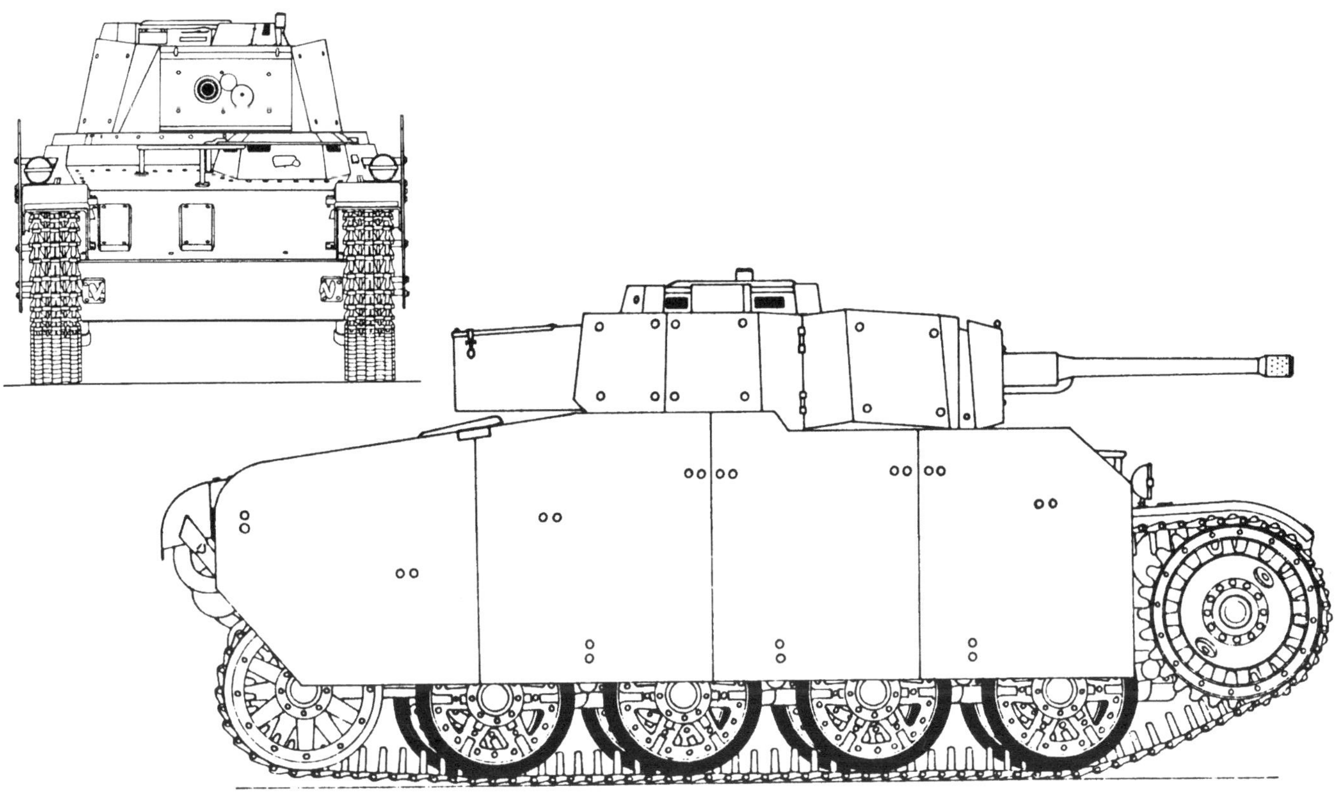

Side sectional view of the 38M Toldi I light tank with the built in engine, weapons in the turret and the transmission system

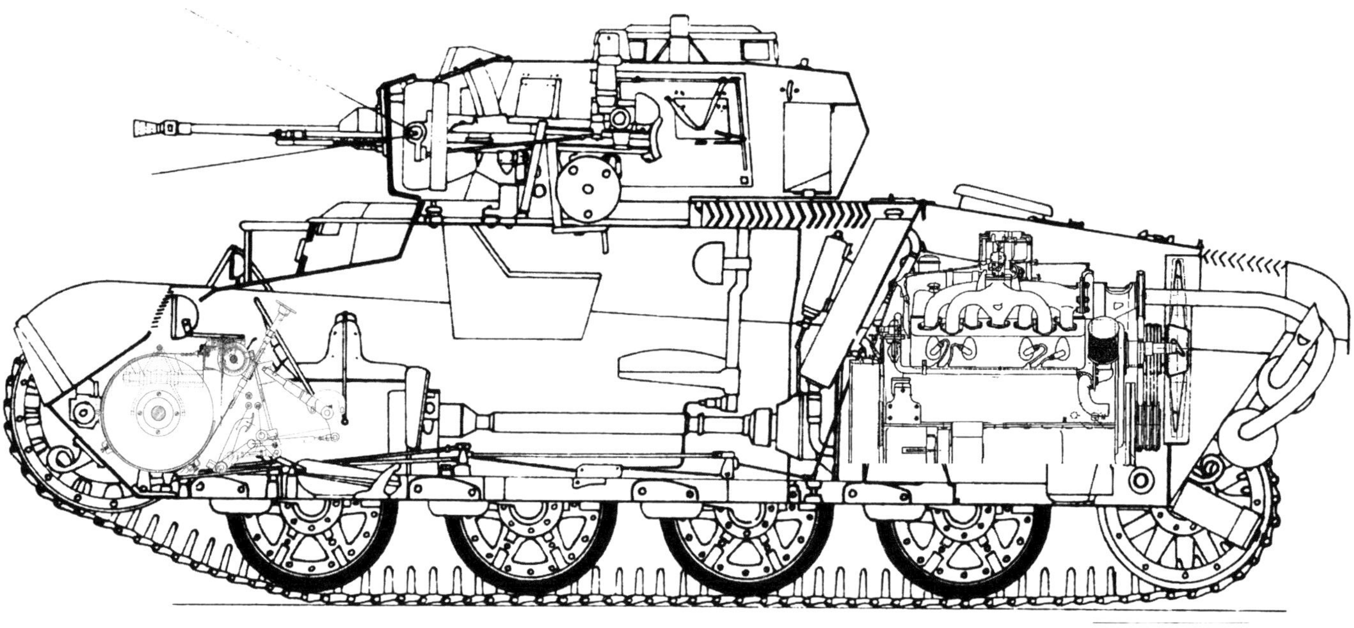

Upper sectional view of the hull, the diagonal position of the engine, the transmission system and the drive shaft is visible

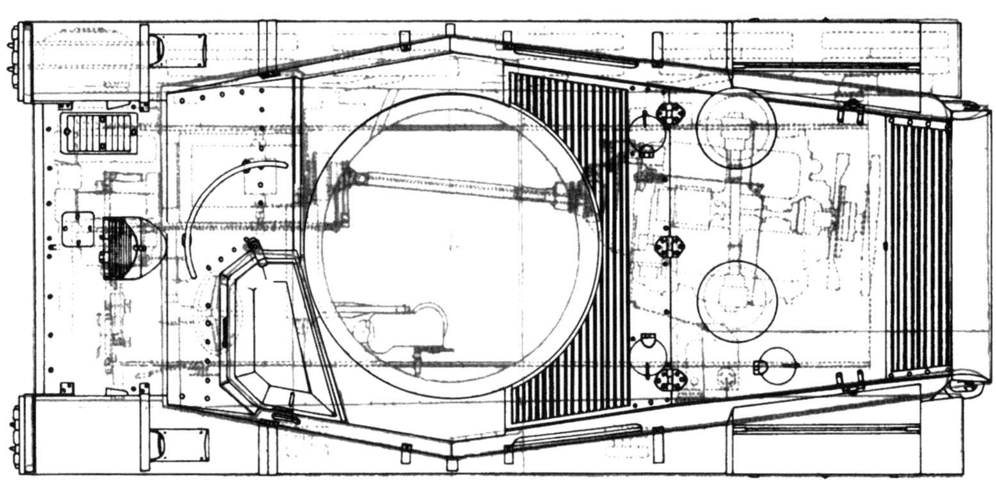

Weapons of the 38M Toldi I light tank [Bajtos Iván]

– 36M 20mm anti-tank rifle with and without scope and upper view

– 34/37M 8mm Gebauer machine gun with 25rounds magazine

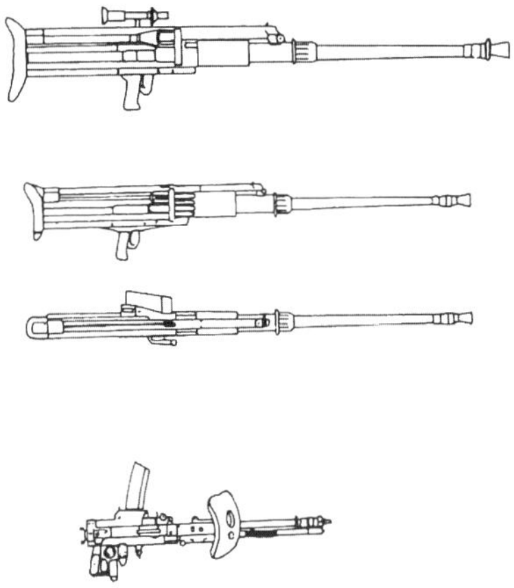

Modification of the turret of the 38M Toldi IIA to housing the 42M 40mm gun [Bajtos Iván]

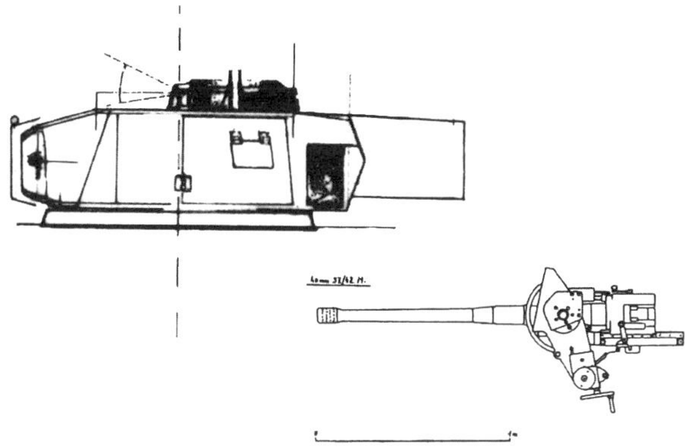

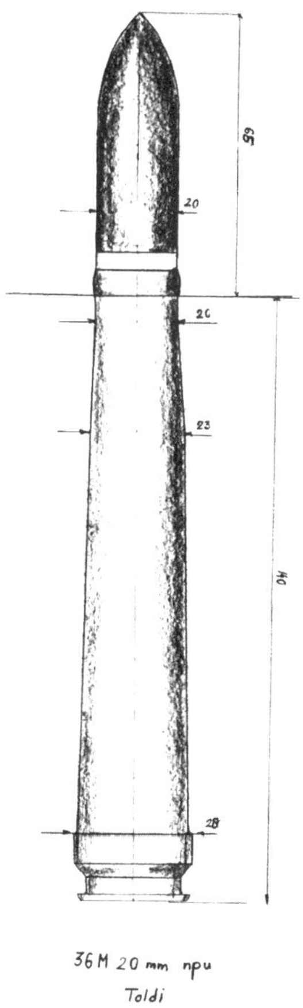

36M 20mm shell for the 36M anti-tank rifle used by the 38M Toldi I light tank [Maintenance Manual]

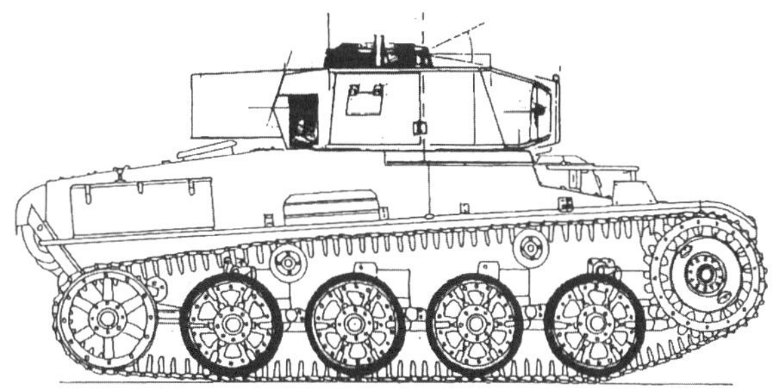

37M 40mm gun used for the V-4 and for the developing the new 38M Toldi IIA [Bajtos Iván]

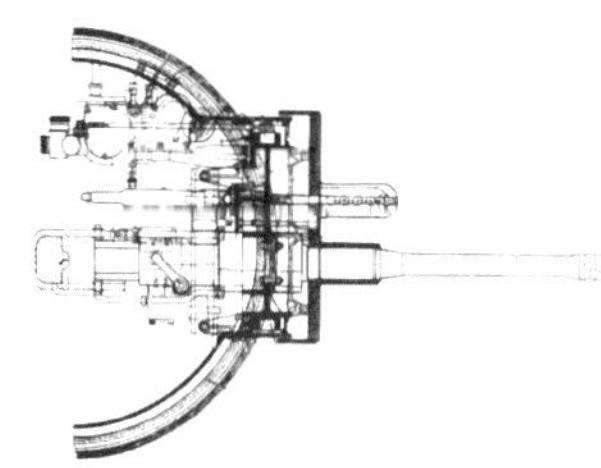

Upper view of the turret of the 38M Toldi IIA with the layout of the weapons [Maintenance Manual]

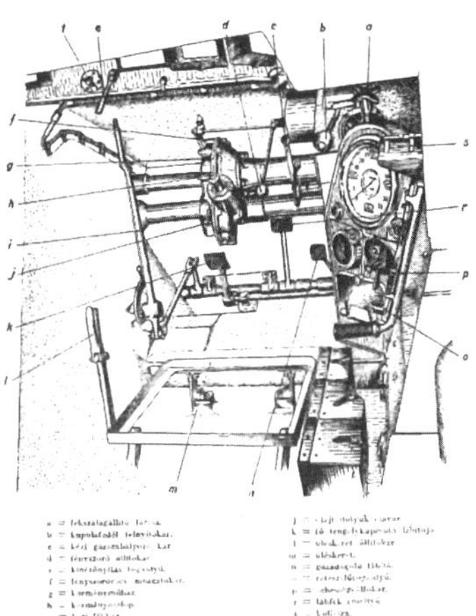

Driver position, the steering wheel could be removed to ease the exiting from the vehicle [Maintenance Manual]

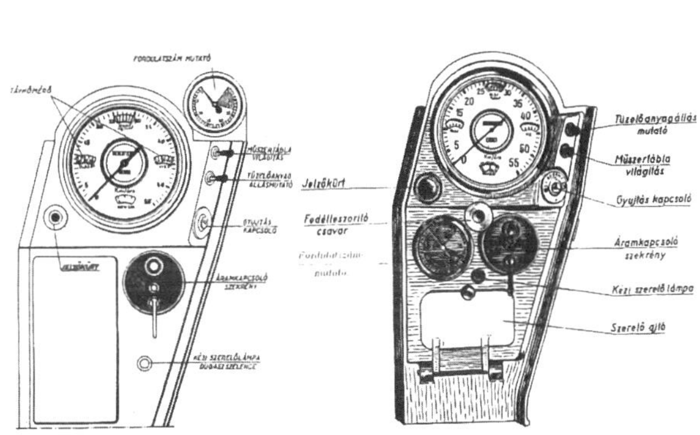

Instrument panel of the driver [Maintenance Manual]

– on the left is the 38M Toldi I light tank instrument panel

– on the right is the 38M Toldi II light tank instrument panel

3D drawing of the steering and chain drive system of the 38M Toldi light tank [Maintenance Manual]

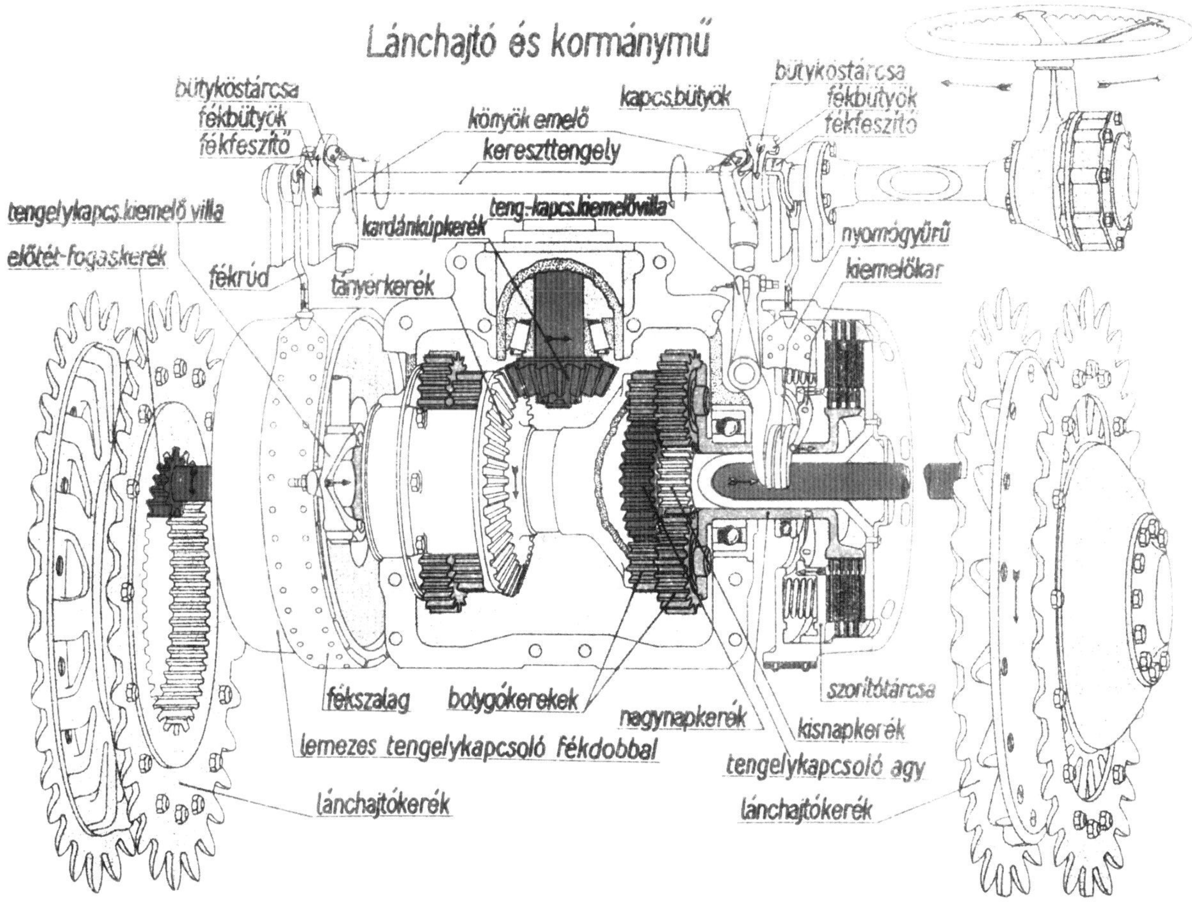

Side view of the chain drive system of the 38M Toldi light tank [Maintenance Manual]

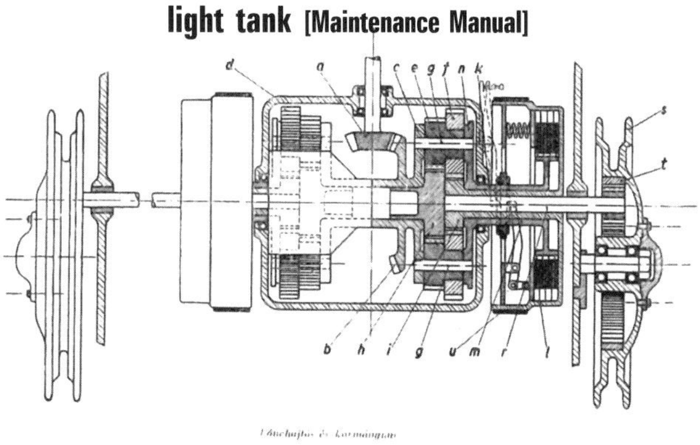

Five view of the 8-liter Bussing-NAG L8V/36TR 155hp engine [Maintenance Manual]

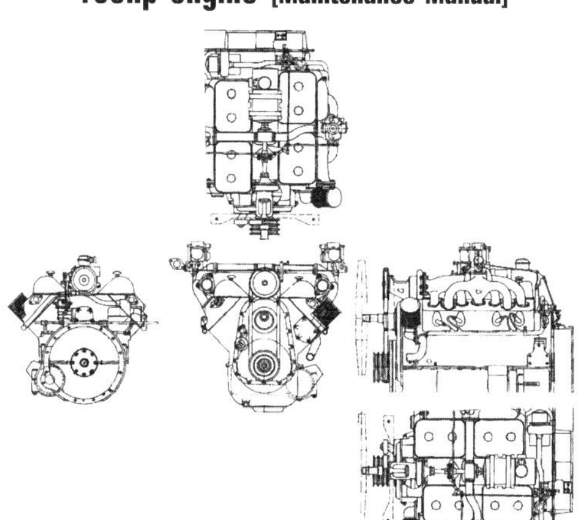

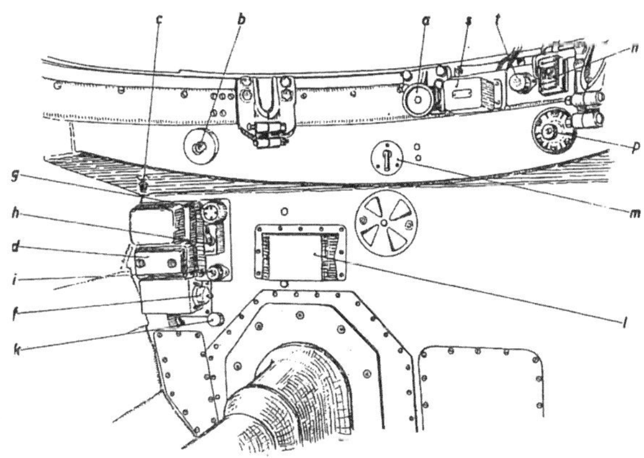

a = toronyrögzítő berendezés.
b = indítóporlasztó húzógombja.
c = külső indításhoz testelés.
d = dinamó feszültségszabályozó és visszáramkapcsoló.
f = 2-es kioldóbiztosíték.
g = külső akkutöltő dugalj.
h = hőkioldó biztosíték.
i = kézi szerelőlámpa dugalj.
k = külső indításhoz kábelszorító (+).
l = burkolat az olajhűtőelzárócsapok lefedésére.
m = tüzelőanyag elzárócsap.
n = 4-es kiolvadó biztosíték.
p = kézi (segéd-) tápszivattyú.
s = R—5a. feszültségszabályozójelfogó
t = távcsöves hk. irányzék dugalj.

Küzdőtér-hátfal szerelvényei.

Rear wall of the fighting compartment of the 38M Toldi light tank with the cover of the drive shaft [Maintenance Manual]

Side view of the position of 60 litters water tank and the cooling system in the engine compartment of the 38M Toldi light tank [Maintenance Manual]

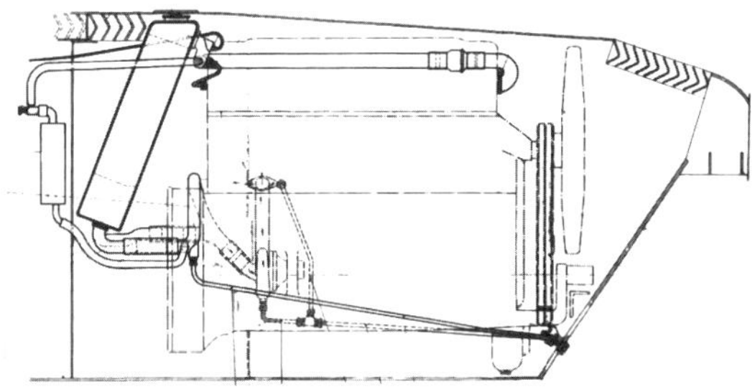

Side view of the position of the Bussing-NAG L8V/36TR and the cooling system with the 60 litters water tank [Maintenance Manual]

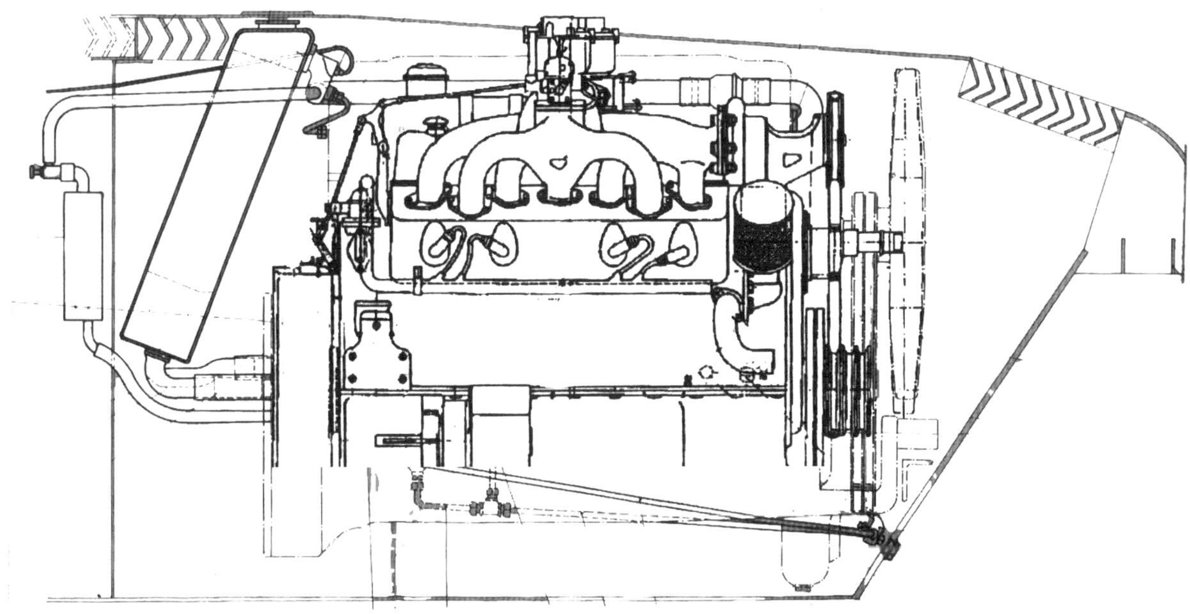

The composition and parts of the track system [Maintenance Manual]

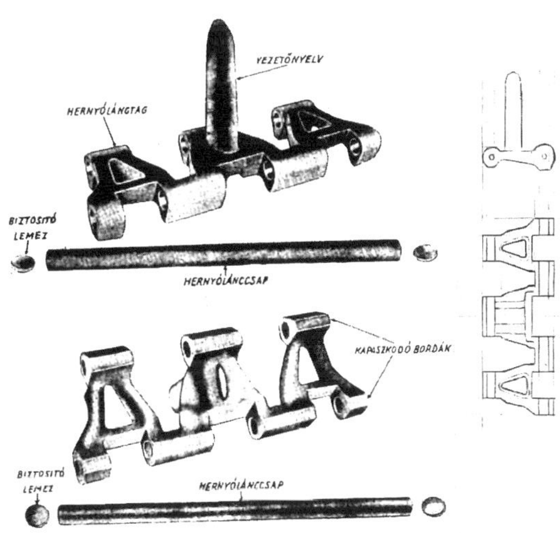

38M Toldi experimental tank hunter [Bajtos Iván]

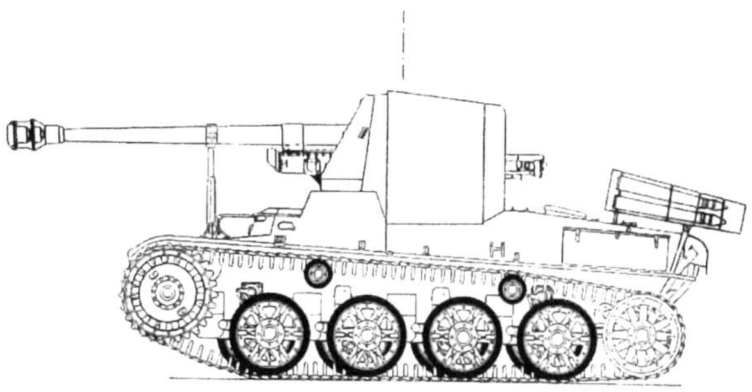

Side view of the 38M Toldi experimental tank hunter with internal ammunition storage bin at the rear of the vehicle

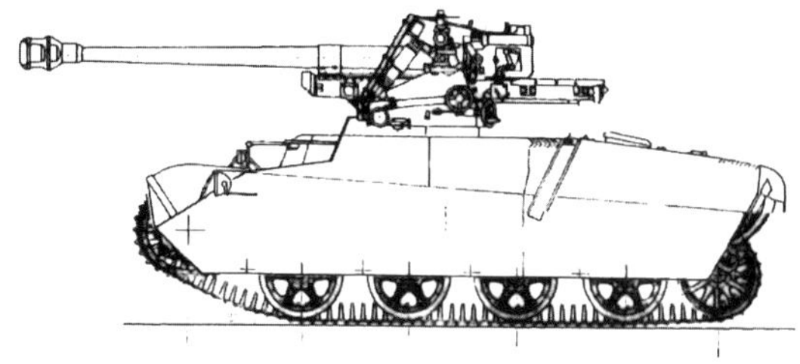

Side sectional view of the vehicles with the borrowed German Pak 40 gun

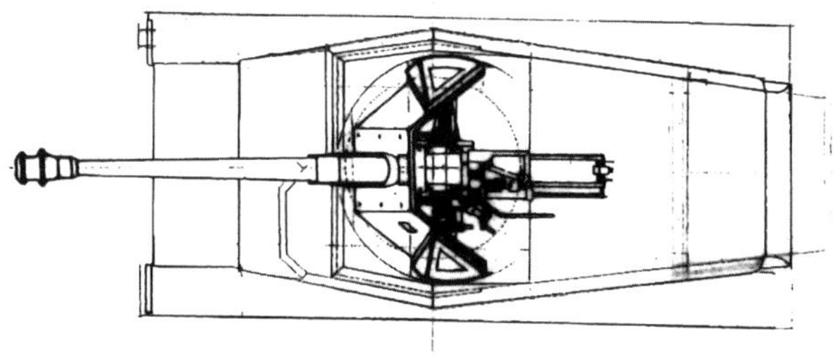

Upper view of the vehicles with its 75mm Pak anti-tank gun

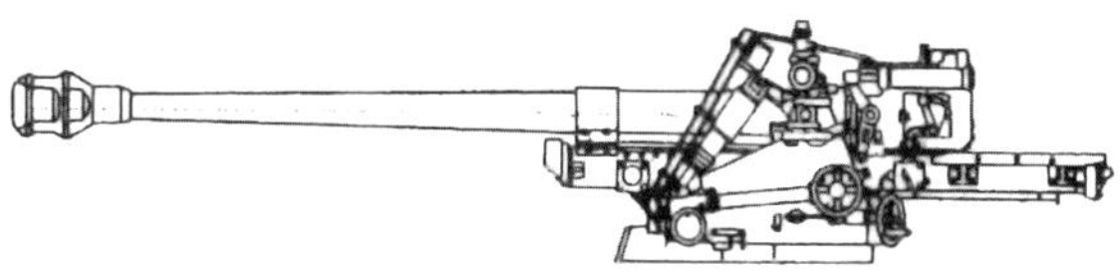

Side view of the 75mm Pak 40 anti-tank gun

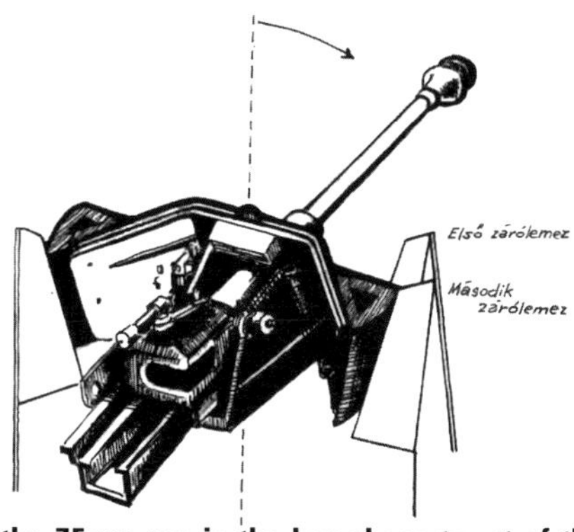

Position of the 75mm gun in the box shape turret of the Toldi tank hunter

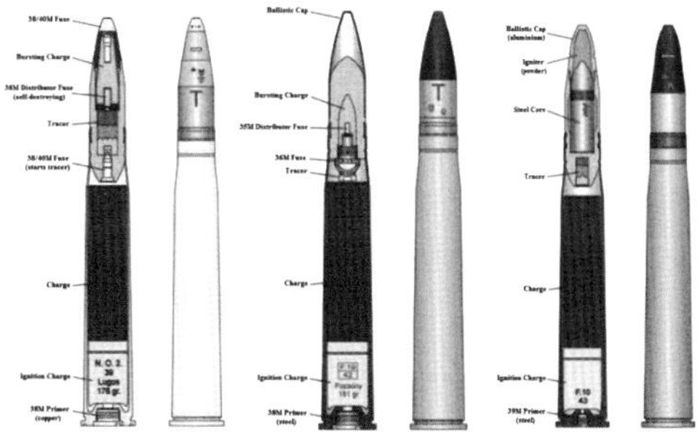

40mm ammunition used by the 40mm 40M anti-tank guns, the 36M Boffors anti aircraft gun, the 40 Turán medium tank as well as the 38M Toldi IIA light tank projectiles from left to right [Service Manual]

- 40mm 39M splinter round
- 40mm 40M AP round
- 40mm 43M APC round experimental

Military insignia and unit signs 1940 – 1944

[colour military and unit insignias from Huns on Wheels, painted by Tamás Deák]

Military insignia

Early military insignia
1st Reconnaissance Battalion
1940 Transylvania

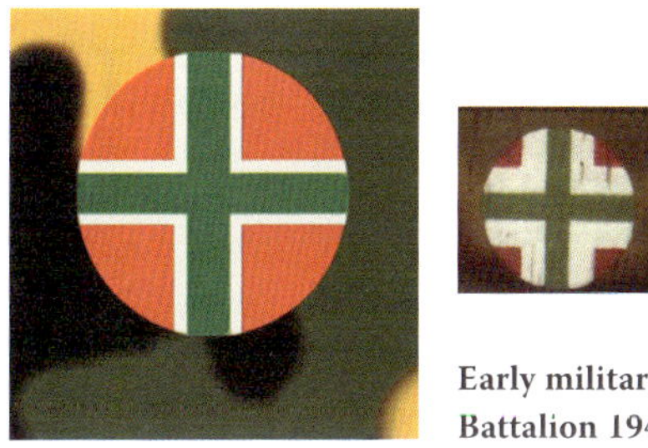

Early military insignia 2nd Reconnaissance Battalion 1940-1941

Octagonal military insignia
Mechanised Branch decals
1941-1942

Late style military insignia
1942-1944

Mechanised Branch decals 1939-1942

Unit signs

1st Reconnaissance Battalion 1940 – 1944

2nd Reconnaissance Battalion 1940 -1941

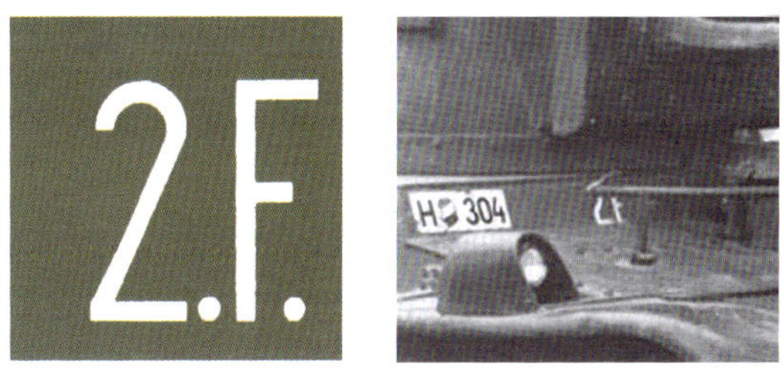

Light Tank Company, 1st Armoured Cavalry Battalion 1940-1941

2nd Reconnaissance Battalion 1941

11th Bicycle – Light Tank Battalion 1941

9th Bicycle – Light Tank Battalion 1941 Ukraine

Armoured Field Battalion 1941 Ukraine

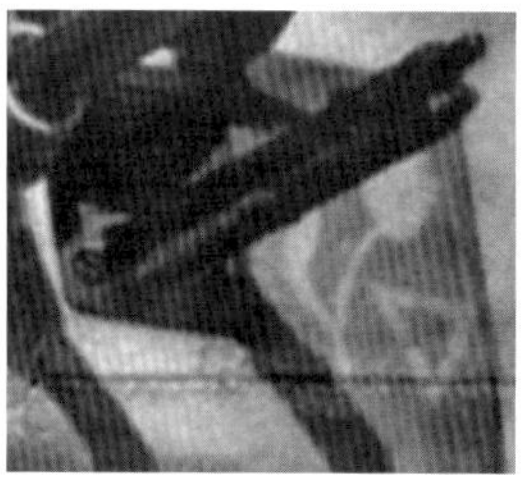

30th Tank Regiment 1942 River Don

51st Sp. AT-AA Battalion 1942 River Don

1/I Tank Battalion 1943-1944

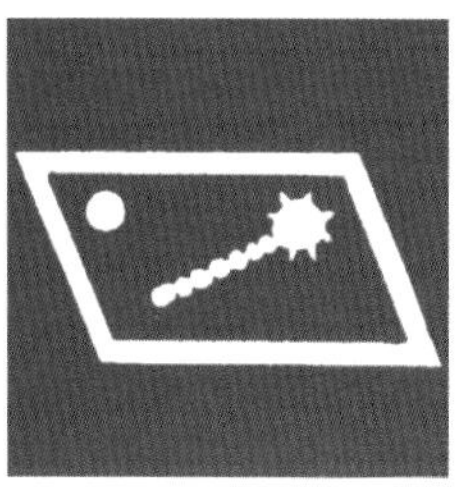

3rd Tank Company 9th Bicycle – Light Tank Battalion 1941 Ukraine

1st Armoured Cavalry Battalion 1941 Ukraine

30/I Tank Battalion 1942 River Don

30/II Tank Battalion 1942 River Don

1st Tank Regiment 1943-1944

1/II Tank Battalion 1943-1944

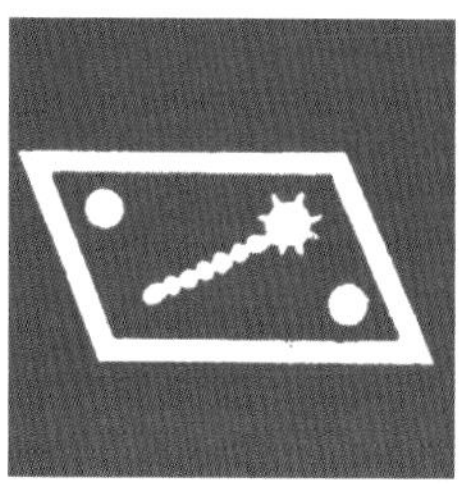

3rd Tank Regiment 1943-1944

3/I Tank Battalion 1943-1944

3/II Tank Battalion 1943-1944

3/III Tank Battalion 1943-1944

52nd Sp. AA Battalion 1943-1944

Companies of the 1st Cavalry Tank Battalion

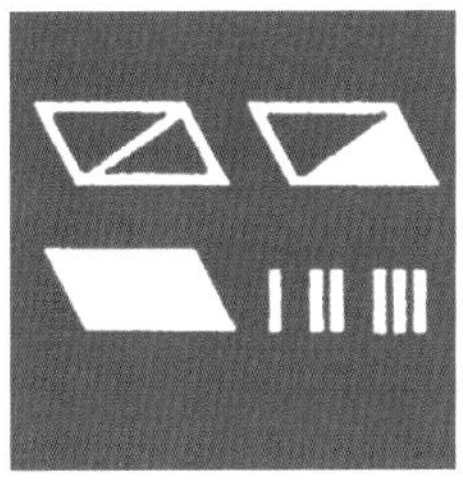

Medium Company of the 1st Cavalry Tank Battalion

Ludovika Military Academy 1940-1944

Painted by Arkadiusz Wróbel

38. M Toldi light tank belonged to the 1. Light Tank Company of the 1. Armoured Cavalry Battalion, September 1940, occupation of Transylvania, white Turul bird with sword was the unit insignia of the light tank company.

38. M Toldi light tank belonged to the 9. Bicycle-Tank Battalion wears the standard octagonal military insignia and next to it the Mechanised Branch insignia on the turret, summer of 1941 Ukraine.

Painted by Arkadiusz Wróbel

38. M Toldi light tank up gunned with 40mm gun, the light tank belonged to the 2. Armoured Division and was captured by Soviet forces in summer of 1944, Galicia. The Toldi light tank has the late war military insignia and three tone camouflage.

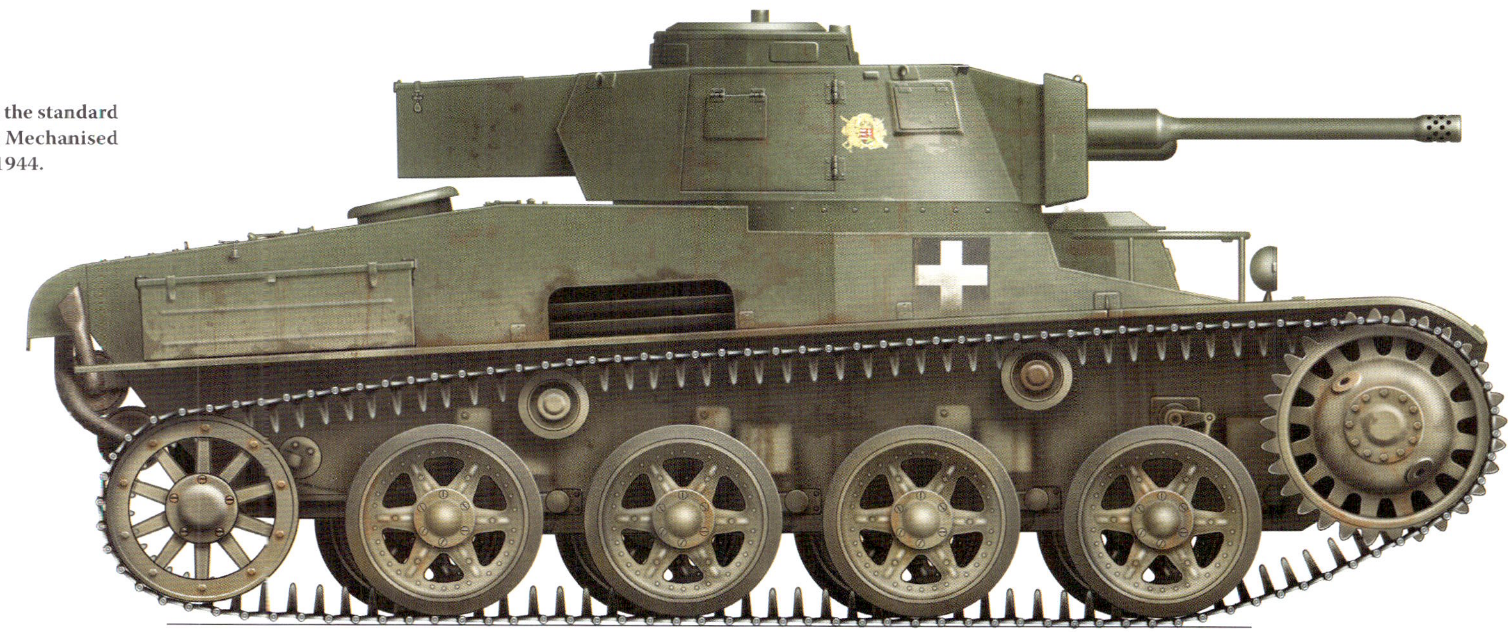

38. M Toldi belonged to the 1. Cavalry Tank Battalion, have the standard olive green camouflage with late style military insignia an Mechanised Branch sign on the turret, in Poland summer of 1944.

Painted by Arkadiusz Wróbel

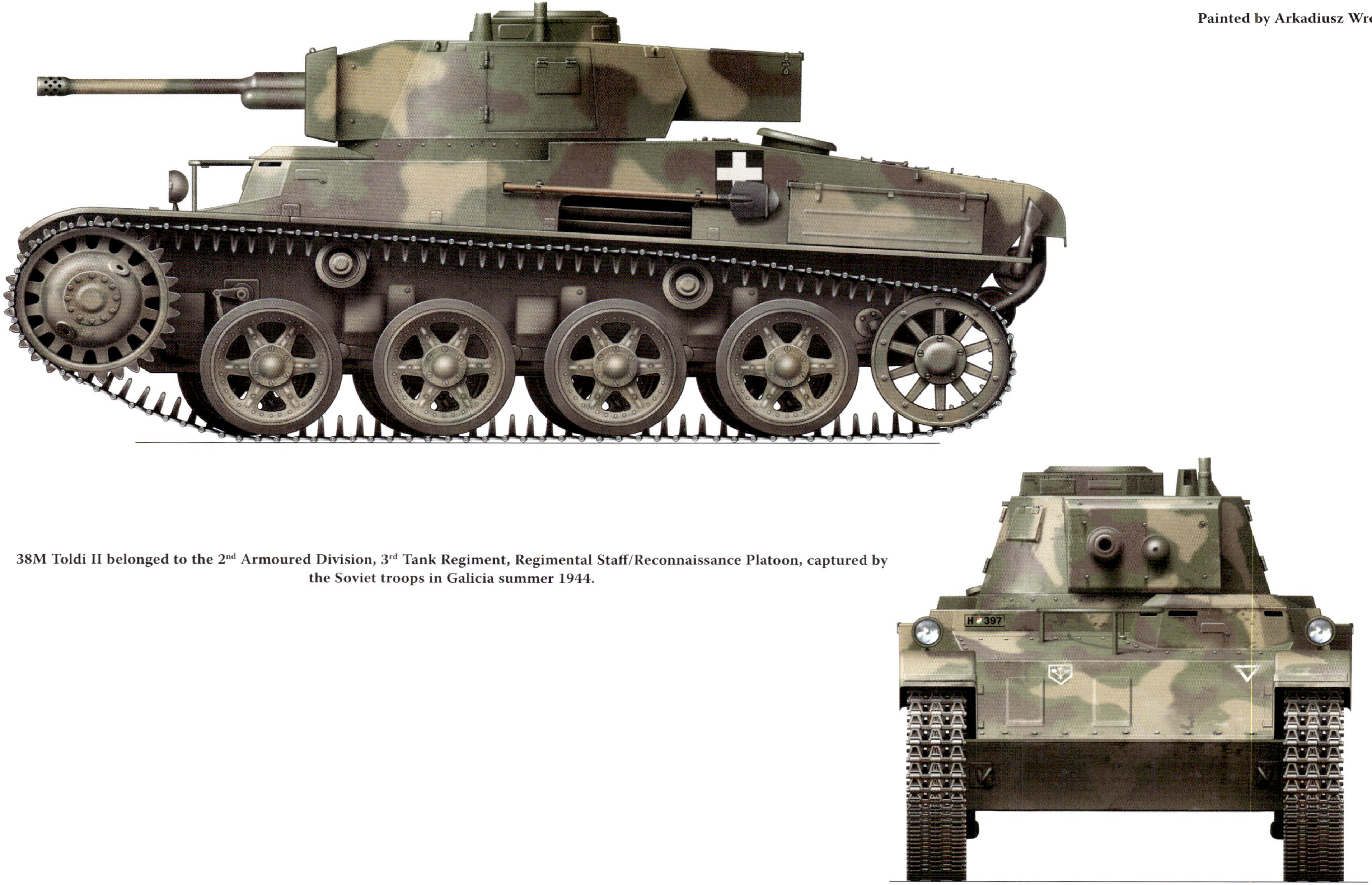

38M Toldi II belonged to the 2nd Armoured Division, 3rd Tank Regiment, Regimental Staff/Reconnaissance Platoon, captured by the Soviet troops in Galicia summer 1944.

Painted by Arkadiusz Wróbel

The upper view of 38M Toldi II belonged to the 2nd Armoured Division, 3rd Tank Regiment, Regimental Staff/Reconnaissance Platoon, captured by the Soviet troops in Galicia.

38M Toldi II tank belonged to the 1. Armoured Division, 1. Tank Regiment in Hungary winter of 1944-1945.

Painted by Arkadiusz Wróbel

38M Toldi light tank without turret during the siege of Budapest 1944-1945 Budapest.